Arabic

Picture Dictionary

Arabic
Picture Dictionary

Berlitz Publishing/APA Publications GmbH & Co. Verlag KG
Singapore Branch, Singapore

The Arabic script is written from right to left (except for numbers); unlike English which is written from left to right. Arabic is a gender-specific language; so words are either 'masculine' (like 'house') or 'feminine' (like 'car'). Words for referring to actions (like 'to sell') may change in form depending on whether you are speaking to a man or a woman. For simplicity, only forms used for talking to a man have been included.

Cover illustration by Chris L. Demarest
Interior illustrations by Chris L. Demarest (pages 3, 5, 7-9, 12-23, 26-43, 46-51, 54-67, 70-75, 78-85, 88-107, and 110-119)
Anna DiVito (pages 24, 25, 52, 53, 76, 77, 86, 87, and 120-123)
Claude Martinot (pages 10, 11, 44, 45, 68, 69, 108, and 109)

Translation and interior layout by Lingua Tech Pte Ltd.
Printed in Singapore by Insight Print Services.

Dear Parents,

The Berlitz Kids™ *Picture Dictionary* will create hours of fun and productive learning for you and your child. Children love sharing books with adults, and reading together is a natural way for your child to develop second-language skills in an enjoyable and entertaining way.

In 1878, Professor Maximilian Berlitz had a revolutionary idea about making language learning accessible and fun. These same principles are still successfully at work today. Now, more than a century later, people all over the world recognize and appreciate his innovative approach. Berlitz Kids™ combines the time-honored traditions of Professor Berlitz with current research to create superior products that truly help children learn foreign languages.

Berlitz Kids™ materials let your child gain access to a second language in a positive way. The content and vocabulary in this book have been carefully chosen by language experts to provide basic words and phrases that form the foundation of a core vocabulary. In addition, the book will delight your child, since each word is used in an amusing sentence in both languages, and then illustrated in an engaging style. The pictures are a great way to capture your child's attention!

You will notice that most words are listed as separate entries. At the back of the book, there are special pages that show words grouped together by theme. For example, if your child is especially interested in animals, he or she will find a special Animals page with lots of words and pictures grouped there–in both English and the foreign language.

The Berlitz Kids™ *Picture Dictionary* has an easy-to-use index at the back of the book. This index lists the English words in alphabetical order and gives the page number where the word appears in the main part of the book.

We hope the Berlitz Kids™ *Picture Dictionary* will provide you and your child with hours of enjoyable learning.

The Editors at Berlitz Kids™

a/an
الـ **al**

A sandwich and an apple are the cat's lunch.

الشطيرة والتفاحة غداء القطة.
alshateera watofaha ghada' al qeta.

across
على الجانب الآخر
aala al janeb alakhar

The fork is across from the spoon.

الشوكة على الجانب الآخر للملعقة.
al shawka 'aala al janeb alakhar lel-mel'aaqa.

to add
يجمع **yajma'a**

I like to add numbers.

أحب جمع الأعداد.
oheb jam'a ala'adad.

adventure
مغامرة **moghamara**

What an adventure!

يالها من مغامرة!
yalaha men moghamara!

afraid
خائف **kha-ef**

The elephant is afraid.

الفيل خائف.
alfeel kha-ef.

after
بعد **ba'ad**

She eats an apple after lunch.

تأكل تفاحة بعد الغداء.
heya ta'kol tofaha ba'ad alghada'.

again
مراراً وتكراراً
meraran wa tekraran

She jumps again and again.

تقفز مراراً وتكراراً.
heya taqfez meraran wa tekraran.

to agree
يتفق **yat-tafeq**

They need to agree.

يجب أن يتفقا.
yajeb an yat-tafeqa.

air
هواء **hawa'**

A balloon is full of air.

البالون مملوء بالهواء.
al ballon mamlo' bel hawa'.

airplane *See Transportation (page 116).*

طائرة **ta-era**

airport

مطار **ma-taar**

Airplanes land at the airport.

الطائرات تهبط في المطار.
al ta-erat tahbet fe almatar.

all

كل **kol**

All the frogs are green.

كل الضفادع خضراء.
kol al dafade'a khadra'.

alligator *See Animals (page 104).*

تمساح **tems-sah**

almost

تقريباً
taqreban

He can almost reach it.

يصل تقريباً.
yassel taqreban.

along

على طول **aala tool**

There are birds along the path.

هناك طيور على طول الطريق.
honak toyor 'aala tool altareeq.

already

بالفعل **belfe'al**

He already has a hat.

عنده قبعة بالفعل.
aendaho qoba'aa belfe'al.

and

و **wa**

I have two sisters and two brothers.

لي أختان وأخان
li okhtan wa akhan.

to answer

يجيب **yojeeb**

Who wants to answer the question?

من يجيب على السؤال؟
mn yojeeb 'aala el so'al?

ant *See Insects (page 110).*
نملة namla

apartment
شقة shaqa

He is in the apartment.

هو في الشقة.
howa fe alshaqa.

apple
تفاح tofah

The apple is falling.

يتساقط التفاح.
yatasaqat altofah.

April
أبريل abreel

The month after
March is April.

الشهر التالي لمارس هو أبريل.
alshahr altali lemares howa abreel.

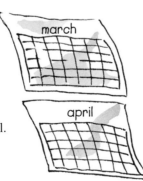

arm *See Parts of the Body (page 114).*
ذراع zera'a

armadillo
حيوان المدرَّع
hayawan almodara'a

Some armadillos live
in Mexico.

تعيش بعض من حيوانات المدرَّع في المكسيك.
ta'aeesh ba'ad men hayawanat almodara'a fe almexceek.

around
حول hawl

Someone is walking around
the stool.

الأرنب يسير حول الكرسي.
alarnab yasseer hawl alkorsi.

art
فن fn

Is it art?

هل هذا فن؟
hal haza fn?

as
مثل methl

He is as tall as a tree!

طويل مثل الشجرة!
taweel methl alshajara!

to ask
يسأل yassa'l

It is time to ask, "Where are my sheep?"

هذا وقت السؤال "أين خرافي؟"
haza waqt al so'al "ayn kherafi?"

aunt
خالة khala

My aunt is my mom's sister.

أخت أمي هي خالتي.
okht omi heya khalati.

at
في fe

The cat is at home.

القطة في المنزل.
alqeta fe almanzel.

awake
يستيقظ yastayqedh

The duck is awake.

البطة تستيقظ.
albata tastayqedh.

August
أغسطس aghostos

The month after July is August.

الشهر التالي ليوليو هو أغسطس.
alshahr altali leyolyo howa aghostos.

away
بعيداً ba'aedan

The cat is going away.

القطة تذهب بعيداً.
alqeta tazhab ba'aedan.

baby

رضيع radee'a

The baby likes to eat bananas.

يحب الرضيع أكل الموز.
yoheb alradee'a akl almawz.

back

ظهر dhahr

She is scratching his back.

هي تحك ظهره.
heya tahok dhahreh.

bad

شرير sher-reer

what a bad, bad monster!

ياله من وحش شرير!
yalaho men wahsh sher-reer!

bag

كيس kees

The bag is full.

الكيس ممتلئ.
alkees momtale'.

bakery

مخبز makhbz

Everything at the bakery smells great!

رائحة كل شيء في المخبز رائعة!
ra-ehat kol shaye' fe almakhbz ra-e'aa!

ball

كرة kora

Can he catch the ball?

هل يمكنه الإمساك بالكرة؟
hal yonkenaho alemsak bel kora?

balloon

بالون ballon

It is a balloon!

إنه بالون!
enaho ballon!

banana

موز mawz

The bananas are in the bowl.

الموز في السلطانية.
almawz fe alsoltaniea.

band

فرقة ferqa

The band is loud.

صوت الفرقة الموسيقية مرتفع.
sawt alferqa almoseqiea mortafe'a.

bandage

ضمادة damada

She has a bandage on her knee.

هي تضع ضمادة على ركبتها.
heya tada'a damada 'aala rokbateha.

coin bank
حصالة **hassala**

Put your money
into the coin bank!

ضع نقودك في الحصالة!
da'a nokodak fe alhassala!

barber
حلاق **hal-laq**

The barber cuts my hair.

يقص الحلاق شعري.
yaqos alhal-laq sha'ari.

to bark
ينبح **yanbah**

Dogs like to bark.

تحب الكلاب أن تنبح.
toheb al kelab an tanbah.

baseball *See Games and Sports (page 108).*
بيسبول **baseball**

basket
سلة **sal-la**

What is in the basket?

ما الذي بداخل السلة؟
ma al-lazi bedakhel alsal-la?

basketball *See Games and Sports (page 108).*
كرة سلة **korat sal-la**

bat
خفاش **khofash**

The bat is sleeping.

الخفاش نائم.
alkhofash na-em.

bat
مضرب **mudrub**

Hit the ball with the bat!

اضرب الكرة بالمضرب!
edrub al kora belmudrub!

bath
استحمام **estehmam**

She is taking a bath.

هي تستحم.
heya tastahem.

to be
يكون **yakon**

Would you like to be my
friend?

هل تحب أن تكون صديقي؟
hal toheb an takon sadeqi?

beach
شاطئ **shate'**

I like to play at the beach.

أحب اللعب على الشاطئ.
oheb al-la'aeb 'aala alshate'.

beans
فول **foul**

He likes to eat beans.

هو يحب أكل الفول.
howa yoheb akl alfoul.

bear *See Animals (page 104).*
دب **dob**

beautiful
جميلة **jameela**

Look at the beautiful things.

انظر إلى الأشياء الجميلة.
ondhor ila alashya' aljameela.

because
لأن **le-an**

She is wet because it is raining.

هي مبتلة لأن السماء ممطرة.
heya mobtal-la le-an alsama' momtera.

bed
سرير **sareer**

The bed is next to the table.

السرير بجوار المنضدة.
alsareer bejewar almendada.

bee *See Insects (page 110).*
نحلة **nahla**

beetle *See Insects (page 110).*
خنفساء **khonfessa'**

before
قبل **qabl**

Put on your socks before you put on your shoes.

البس الجورب قبل لبس الحذاء.
elbes aljawrub qabl lebs alheza'.

to begin
يبدأ **yabd'**

She wants to begin the painting.

هي أرادت أن تبدأ الطلاء.
heya aradat an tabda' altelaa'.

behind
خلف **khalf**

The boy is behind the tree.

الولد خلف الشجرة.
alwalad khalf alshajara.

to believe
يصدق **yosadeq**

This is too good to believe.

شيء لا يصدقه عقل.
shay' la yosadeqoh 'aaql.

bell
جرس **jaras**

Don't ring that bell!

لا تدق هذا الجرس!
la tadoq haza aljaras!

belt *See Clothing (page 106).*
حزام **hezam**

berry
توت **tout**

Those berries look good.

هذا التوت لذيذ.
haza altout laziz.

best
أفضل **afdul**

The red box is the best.

الصندوق الأحمر هو الأفضل.
alsandooq alahmar howa alafdul.

better
أحسن **ahsn**

The belt is better than the pin.

الحزام أحسن من الدبوس.
alhezam ahsn men aldoboos.

between
بين **bayn**

He is between two trees.

هو بين الشجرتين.
howa bayn alshajaratien.

bicycle *See Transportation (page 116).*
دراجة **daraja**

big
كبير **kabeer**

He is very big.

هو كبير جداً.
howa kabeer jedan.

biking *See Games and Sports (page 108).*

ركوب الدراجة rokob aldaraja

bird

طائر ta-er

The bird is flying south for the winter.

يطير الطائر نحو الجنوب لقضاء الشتاء.
yateer alta-er naho al janoob leqada' alsheta'.

birthday

عيد ميلاد aeed melad

Happy birthday!

عيد ميلاد سعيد!
aeed melad sa'aeed!

black *See Numbers and Colors (page 112).*

أسود aswad

blank

خالي khali

The pages are blank.

الصفحات خالية.
alsafahat khali-ya.

blanket

بطانية batanya

What is under that blanket?

ما الذي تحت البطانية؟
ma al-lazi taht albatanya?

blouse *See Clothing (page 106).*

قميص qamees

to blow

تهب tahoob

The wind is starting to blow.

بدأت الرياح في الهبوب.
bada'at alreyah fe alhoboob.

blue *See Numbers and Colors (page 112).*

أزرق azraq

boat *See Transportation (page 116).*

قارب qareb

book

كتاب ketab

I am reading a book.

أنا أقرأ كتاب.
ana aqra' ketab.

bookstore

مكتبة maktaba

You can buy a book at a bookstore.

يمكنك شراء كتاب من المكتبة.
yomkenak shera' ketab men almaktaba.

boots *See Clothing (page 106).*
أحذية ah-zia

bottle
زجاجة zojaja

The straw is in the bottle.

الماصة في الزجاجة.
almassa fe alzojaja.

bowl
سلطانية soltanya

Some food is still in the bowl.

الطعام مازال في السلطانية.
al ta'aam mazal fe alsoltanya.

bowling *See Games and Sports (page 108).*
بولينغ balling

box
صندوق sondooq

Why is that fox in the box?

لماذا هذا الثعلب داخل الصندوق؟
lemaza haza alta'alab dakhel alsondooq?

boy
ولد walad

The boys are twin brothers.

الولدان أخوان توأمان.
alwaladan akhawan taw-aman.

16

branch
فرع far'a

Oh, no! Get off that branch!

لا! ابتعد عن الفرع!
la! ebta'aed 'aan alfar'a!

brave
شجاع sjoja'a

What a brave mouse!

ياله من فأر شجاع!
yalaho men fa'r shoja'a!

bread
خبز khobz

He likes bread with jam and butter.

هو يحب الخبز مع المربى والزبدة.
howa yoheb alkhobz ma'aa almoraba wazobda.

to break
يكسر yaksar

It is easy to break an egg.

من السهل كسر البيضة.
men alsahl kasr albayda.

breakfast
فطور fotoor

Morning is the time for breakfast.

الصباح هو وقت تناول الفطور.
alsabah howa waqt tanawol alfotoor.

bridge
جسر **jesr**

The boat is under the bridge.

القارب تحت الجسر.
alqareb taht aljesr.

to bring
يجلب **yajleb**

She wants to bring the lamb to school.

هي أرادات أن تجلب الحمل إلى المدرسة.
heya aradat an tajleb al hamal ila almadrassa.

broom
مكنسة **maknassa**

A broom is for sweeping.

المكنسة تكنس.
almaknassa taknos.

brother
أخ **akh**

He is my brother.

هو أخي.
howa akhi.

brown *See Numbers and Colors (page 112).*
بني **bon-nee**

brush
فرشاة **forsha**

I need my hairbrush.

أريد فرشاة شعري.
oreed forashat sha'ari.

bubble
فقاعة **foqa'a**

The bathtub is full of bubbles.

حوض الاستحمام ممتلئ بالفقاعات.
hawd alestehmam momtale' belfoqa'aat.

bug
حشرة **hashara**

Do you know the name of this bug?

هل تعرف اسم هذه الحشرة؟
hal ta'aref esm hazehi alhashara?

to build
يبني **yabni**

I want to build a box.

أريد بناء صندوقاً.
oreed bena' sondooqan.

B

bus *See Transportation (page 116).*
حافلة hafela

bush
شجيرة shojiera

A bird is in the bush.

الطائر على الشجيرة.
alta-er 'aal alshojiera.

busy
مشغول mash-ghool

He is very busy.

هو مشغول جداً.
howa mash-ghool jedan.

but
لكن laken

The pencil is on the table,
but the book is on the chair.

القلم الرصاص على المنضدة ولكن
الكتاب على الكرسي.
alqalam alrassas 'aal almendada
walaken alketab 'aala alkorsi.

butter
زبدة zobda

Bread and butter
taste good.

الخبز بالزبدة لذيذ الطعم.
alkhbz belzobda laziz alta'am.

butterfly *See Insects (page 110).*
فراشة farasha

button
زر zer

One button is missing.

هناك زر مفقود.
honak zer mafqood.

to buy
يشتري yashtaree

He wants to buy
a banana.

هو يريد شراء موزة.
howa yoreed shera' mawza.

by
إلى جانب ila janeb

She is standing
by the cheese.

هي تقف إلى جانب الجبن.
heya taqef ila janeb aljobn.

cage
قفص qafas

The bird is on the cage.

الطائر فوق القفص.
alta-er fawq alqafas.

cake
كعكة ka'aka

She likes to eat cake.

هي تحب أكل الكعكة.
heya toheb akl alka'aka.

to call
يتصل yatasel

Remember to call me again later.

تذكر الاتصال بي في وقت لاحق.
tazakar an tatassel be fe waqt laheq.

camel
جمل jamal

The camel is hot.

الجمل حران.
aljamal haran.

camera
كاميرا camera

Smile at the camera!

ابتسم للكاميرا!
ebtassem lelcamera!

can
صفيحة safeha

What is in that can?

ما الذي في الصفيحة؟
ma al-lazi fe alsafeha?

candle
شمعة sham'aa

She is lighting the candle.

هي تشعل الشمعة.
heya tosh'ael alsham'aa.

candy
حلوى halwa

Candy is sweet.

الحلوى لذيذة.
alhalwa laziza.

cap See Clothing (page 106).
قبعة qoba'aa

car *See Transportation (page 116).*

سيارة sayara

card

بطاقة betaqa

Do you want to play cards?

هل تريد لعب لعبة البطاقات؟
hal toreed la'aeb lo'abat albetaqat?

to care

يعتني ya'atani

Her job is to care for pets.

وظيفتها أن تعتني بالحيوانات الأليفة.
wazefateha an ta'atani belhayawanat alalefa.

carpenter

نجار najar

A carpenter makes things with wood.

النجار يصنع الأشياء من الخشب.
alnajar yasna'a alashya' men alkhashab.

carrot

جزر jazar

A carrot is orange.

الجزر برتقالي.
aljazar bortoqali.

to carry

يحمل yahmel

He carries a big bag.

هو يحمل كيساً كبيراً.
howa yahmel kessan kabeeran.

castanets

صّجات sajat

Click the castanets to the music!

دق الصّجات لتخرج الموسيقى!
doq alsajat letakhroj almosseqa!

castle

قلعة qal'aa

The king lives in a castle.

يعيش الملك في القلعة.
ya'aeesh almalek fe alqal'aa.

cat

قطة qeta

The cat sees the mouse.

القطة ترى الفأر.
alqeta tara al fa'r.

caterpillar *See Insects (page 110).*

يُسروع yosro'a

to catch

يمسك yamsek

He runs to catch the ball.

هو يجري ليمسك الكرة.
howa yajri lemsek alkora.

cave

كهف kahf

Who lives in the cave?

من يعيش في الكهف؟
mn ya'aeesh fe alkahf?

to celebrate

يحتفل yahtafel

They celebrate his birthday.

هم يحتفلوا بعيد ميلاده.
hom yahtafelo be'aed meladeh.

chair

كرسي korsie

He is sitting on a chair.

هو يجلس على كرسي.
howa yajles 'aala alkorsie.

chalk

طباشير tabasheer

you can write with chalk.

يمكنك الكتابة بالطباشير.
yomkenak alketaba beltabasheer.

to change

يغير yoghaier

He wants to change his shirt.

هو يريد أن يغير قميصه.
howa yoreed an yoghaier qameseh.

to cheer

يشجع yoshaje'a

It is fun to cheer for our team.

شيء جميل أن نشجع فريقنا.
shay' jameel an noshaje'a fareqana.

cheese

جبن jobn

The mouse likes to eat cheese.

يحب الفأر أكل الجبن.
yoheb alfa'r akl aljobn.

cherry
كرز **karaz**

He wants a cherry.

هو يريد كرزة.
howa yoreed karaza.

chicken *See Animals (page 104).*
دجاج **dajaj**

child
طفل **tefl**

She is a happy child.

هي طفلة سعيدة.
heya tefla sa'aeda.

chocolate
شوكولاتة **shocolata**

He likes chocolate.

هو يحب الشوكولاتة.
howa yoheb alshocolata.

circle
دائرة **da-era**

It is drawing a circle.

هو يرسم دائرة.
howa yarsem da-era.

circus
سيرك **serk**

There are clowns at a circus.

هناك مهرجين في السيرك.
honak mohrjeen fe alserk.

city
مدينة **madina**

This cow does not live in the city.

البقرة لا تعيش في المدينة.
albaqara la ta'aesh fe almadina.

to clap
يصفق **yo-safeq**

He likes to clap when he is happy.

هو يحب أن يصفق عندما يكون سعيداً.
howa yoheb an yo-safeq 'aendama yakon sa'aedan.

class
فصل **fasl**

There is an elephant in my class.

هناك فيل في فصلي.
honak feel fe fasli.

classroom

فصل دراسي **fasl derassi**

A teacher works in a classroom.

يدرس المعلم في الفصل الدراسي.
yodares almo'aalem fe alfasl derassi.

clean

نظيف **nadheef**

The car is very clean.

السيارة نظيفة جداً.
alsayara nadheefa jedan.

to clean

ينظف **yonadhef**

He is starting to clean his room.

هو يبدأ في تنظيف غرفته.
howa yabda' fe tandheef ghorfateh.

to climb

يتسلق **yata-salq**

The bear likes to climb the tree.

يحب الدب أن يتسلق الشجرة.
yoheb aldob an yata-salq alshajara.

clock

ساعة **sa'aa**

A clock tells time.

الساعة تخبر عن الوقت.
alsa'aa tokhber 'aan al waqt.

close

قريب **qareeb**

The turtle is close to the rock.

السلحفاة قريبة من الصخرة.
alsolahfah qareeba men alshajara.

to close

يقفل **yaqfel**

He is going to close the window.

هو سيقفل النافذة.
howa sayaqfel alnafeza.

cloud

سحاب **sah-hab**

The sun is behind the cloud.

الشمس خلف السحاب.
alshams khalf alah-hab.

clown

مهرج moharej

The clown is funny.

المهرج مضحك.
almoharej mod-heq.

coat *See Clothing (page 106).*

معطف me'ataf

cold

بارد bared

It is cold in here!

الجو بارد هنا!
aljaw bared hona!

comb

مشط mesht

Where is my comb?

أين مشطي؟
ayn mshty?

to comb

يمشط yomashet

He likes to comb his hair.

هو يحب أن يمشط شعره.
howa yoheb an yomashet sha'areh.

to come

يأتي ya'ti

My friends have come to visit me.

أتى أصدقائي لزيارتي.
ata asdeqa-e lezeyaraty.

computer

كمبيوتر computer

She is working at her computer.

هي تعمل على الكمبيوتر.
heya ta'amal 'aala alcomputer.

to cook

يطهو yat-hoo

It is fun to cook.

الطهي شيء لطيف.
altahie shay' lateef.

cookie

كعك ka'ak

Mary wants a cookie.

هي تريد كعكة.
heya toreed ka'aka.

to count

يعد ya'aed

There are too many stars to count.

هناك عدد كبير جداً من النجوم للعد.
honak 'aadad kabeer jedan men alnojom lel'aad.

country

ريف reef

The country is beautiful.

الريف جميل.
alreef jameel.

cow *See Animals (page 104).*

بقرة baqara

crayon

قلم شمع qalm sham'a

She is drawing with her crayons.

هي ترسم بقلمها الشمع.
heya tarsem beqalameha alsham'a.

cricket *See Games and Sports (page 108).*

لعبة الكريكيت lo'abat alcrekit.

cricket *See Insects (page 110).*

صرصار الليل sorsar al-layl

crowded

مزدحم mozdahim

This elevator is crowded.

هذا المصعد مزدحم.
haza almes'aad mozdahim.

to cry

يبكي yabkee

Try not to cry!

حاول ألا تبكي!
hawel ala tabkee!

cup

فنجان finjaan

He is drinking water from the cup.

هو يشرب الماء من الفنجان.
howa yashrab alma' men alfinjaan.

to cut

يقطع yaqta'

Use a knife to cut the carrots!

استخدم سكين لتقطيع الجزر!
estakhdem sek-keen letaqtee'a aljazar!

cute

وسيم wasseem

She thinks her baby is cute.

هي تظن أن رضيعها وسيم.
heya tadhon an rade'aaha wasseem.

D

dad

أبي abi

My dad and I look alike.

أنا وأبي نشبه بعضنا.
ana wa abi noshbeh ba'adana.

to dance

يرقص yarqos

The rabbit likes to dance and play the drum.

يحب الأرنب الرقص ودق الطبلة.
yoheb alarnab alraqs wa daq altabla.

danger

خطر khatar

He is in danger.

هو في خطر.
howa fe khatar.

dark

مظلم modhlem

It is dark at night.

السماء مظلمة في الليل.
alsama' modhlema fe al-layl.

day

نهار nahar

The sun shines in the day.

الشمس تسطع في النهار.
alshams tasta'a fe alnahar.

December

ديسمبر december

The month after November is December.

الشهر التالي لنوفمبر هو ديسمبر.
alshahr altali lenovember howa december.

to decide

يقرر yoqarer

It is hard to decide.

يقرر بصعوبة.
yoqarer beso'aoba.

decision

قرار qarar

That is a good decision.

هذا قرار صحيح.
haza qarar saheh.

decorations

زينة zena

The decorations look great!

الزينة تبدو رائعة!
alzena tabdo ra'e'aa!

deer
غزال **ghazal**

The deer is running
in the woods.

الغزال يركض في الغابة.
alghazal yarkod fe alghaba.

dentist
طبيب أسنان **tabeeb asnan**

The dentist has a big job.

طبيب الأسنان عنده عمل كثير.
tabeeb alasnan 'aendaho 'aamal
katheer.

department
قسم **qesm**

This is the hat department.

هذا هو قسم القبعات.
haza howa qesm alqoba'at.

desk
مكتب **maktab**

The desk is very messy.

مكتب غير مرتب.
maktab ghayr moratb.

different
مختلف **mokhtalef**

The one in the middle
is different.

السمكة الموجودة في المنتصف
مختلفة.
alsamaka almawjoda fe
almontasaf mokhtalefa.

difficult
صعب **sa'ab**

This is difficult!

هذه مسألة صعبة!
hazehi mas'ala sa'aba!

to dig
يحفر **yahfor**

A dog uses its paws to dig.

يستخدم الكلب كفيه ليحفر.
yastakhdem alkalb kafayh
leyahfor.

dinner
عشاء **aasha'**

We have dinner at 6 o'clock.

نتناول العشاء الساعة 6.
natanawal al'aasha' alsa'aa 6.

dinosaur
ديناصور **dinasoor**

The dinosaur is having fun.

الديناصور يمرح.
aldinasoor yamrah.

D

dirty
قذر qazer

The dog is dirty.

الكلب قذر.
alkalb qazer.

dish
طبق tabaq

Do not drop the dishes!

لا تسقط الأطباق!
la tosqet alatbaq!

to do
ينجز yonjez

He has a lot to do.

لديه الكثير لإنجازه.
ladyh alkatheer le-enjazeh.

doctor
طبيب tabeeb

The doctor checks the baby.

الطبيب يفحص الرضيع.
altabeeb yafhas alradee'a.

dog
كلب kalb

The dog has a funny hat.

الكلب يضع قبعة مضحكة.
alkalb yada'a qoba'aa modheka.

doll
دمية domya

The doll is in a box.

الدمية في الصندوق.
aldomya fe alsondooq.

dolphin
درفيل darfeel

Dolphins live in the sea.

تعيش الدرافيل في البحر.
ta'aeesh aldarafeel fe albahr.

donkey
حمار hemar

The donkey is sleeping.

الحمار نائم.
alhemar na-em.

door
باب bab

What is behind the door?

ما الذي خلف الباب؟
ma al-lazi khalf albab?

down
أسفل asfl

The elevator is going down.

المصعد يتجه لأسفل.
almes'aad yatajeh le-asfl.

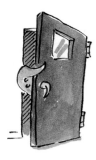

dragon
تنين ten-neen

The dragon is cooking lunch.

التنين يطهو الغداء.
alten-neen yat-hoo alghada'.

to draw
يرسم yarsim

He likes to draw.

هو يحب أن يرسم.
howa yoheb an yarsim.

drawing
رسم rasm

Look at my drawing!

انظر إلى رسمي!
ondhor ila rasmi!

dress *See Clothing (page 106).*
فستان fostan

to drink
يشرب yashrab

She likes to drink milk.

هي تحب أن تشرب الحليب.
heya toheb an tashrab alhaleeb.

to drive
يقود yaqood

He is too small to drive.

هو قصير جداً على القيادة.
howa qaseer jedan 'aala alqeyada.

to drop
يسقط yasqet

He is going to drop the pie.

هو سيسقط الفطيرة.
howa sa-yosqet alfatera.

drum
طبلة tabla

He plays the drum.

هو يدق الطبلة.
howa yadoq altabla.

dry
جاف jaf

The shirt is dry.

القميص جاف.
alqamees jaf.

duck *See Animals (page 104).*
بطة bat-ta

dust
تراب torab

There is dust under the bed.

هناك تراب تحت السرير.
honak torab taht alsareer.

E

each

كل kol

Each snowflake is different.

كل كتلة رقيقة من الثلج مختلفة.
kol kotla raqeqa men althalj
mokhtalefa.

ear *See Parts of the Body (page 114).*

أذن ozon

early

مبكر mobaker

The sun comes up early in the day.

تشرق الشمس مبكراً في النهار.
tashroq alshams mobakeran
fe alnahar.

earmuffs *See Clothing (page 106).*

أغطية الأذن aghtiet alozon

to earn

يكسب yaksab

We work to earn money.

نحن نعمل لنكسب المال.
nahno na'amal lenaksab almal.

east

الشرق alsharq

The sun comes up in the east.

تشرق الشمس من الشرق.
tashroq alshams men alsharq.

to eat

يأكل ya'kol

This bird likes to eat worms.

يحب الطائر أكل الديدان.
yoheb alta-er akl alde-dan.

egg

بيض bayd

The hen has an egg.

الدجاجة تبيض.
aldajaja ta-beed.

eight *See Numbers and Colors (page 112).*

ثمانية thamania

eighteen *See Numbers and Colors (page 112).*

ثمانية عشر thamayat 'aashr

eighty *See Numbers and Colors (page 112).*

ثمـانون thamanoon

elephant *See Animals (page 104).*

فيل feel

eleven *See Numbers and Colors (page 112).*

أحد عشر ahad 'aashr

empty فارغ faregh

The bottle is empty.

الزجاجة فارغة.
alzojaja faregha.

to end
ينهي **yanhi**

It is time to end the game.

حان وقت إنهاء اللعبة.
han waqt enha' allo'aba.

everything
كل شيء **kol shay'**

Everything is purple.

كل شيء بنفسجي.
kol shay' banafseji.

enough
كافي **kafi**

He has enough food!

هو معه طعام كاف!
howa ma'aho ta'aam kaf!

everywhere
كل مكان **kol makan**

There are balls everywhere.

هناك كرات في كل مكان.
honak korat fe kol makan.

every
كل **kol**

Every egg is broken.

كل البيض مكسور.
kol albayd maksoor.

excited
متحمس **mota-hames**

He is excited.

هو متحمس.
howa mota-hames.

everyone
كل شخص **kol shakhs**

Everyone here has spots!

كل شخص عنده نقاط!
kol shakhs 'aendaho neqat!

eye *See Parts of the Body (page 114).*
عين **ayen**

F

face *See Parts of the Body (page 114).*

وجه wajh

factory

مصنع masna'a

Cans are made in this factory.

العلب تصنع في المصنع.
al'aolab tosana'a fe almasna'a.

to fall

يسقط yasqot

He is about to fall.

هو على وشك أن يسقط.
howa 'aala washk an yasqot.

fall

الخريف alkhareef

It is fall.

هذا فصل الخريف.
haza fasl alkhareef.

family

أسرة osra

This is a big family.

هذه أسرة كبيرة.
hazehi osra kabeera.

fan

مروحة merwaha

Please, turn off the fan!

من فضلك أوقف المروحة!
men fadlek awqef almerwaha!

far

بعيد ba'aeed

The moon is far away.

القمر بعيد.
alqamar ba'aeed.

faraway

بعيد جداً ba'aeed jedan

She is going to a faraway place.

هي ذاهبة إلى مكان بعيد جداً.
heya zaheba ila makan ba'aeed jedan.

fast

سريع saree'a

That train is going fast!

هذا القطار سريع جداً!
haza alqetar saree'a jedan!

fat

سمين sa-meen

The rhino is fat.

وحيد القرن سمين.
waheed alqarn sa-meen.

father
أب ab

My father and I look alike.

أنا وأبي نشبه بعضنا.
ana wa abi noshbeh ba'adana.

favorite
مفضل mofadul

This is my favorite toy.

هذه لعبتي المفضلة.
hazehi lo'abati almofadula.

feather
ريش reesh

The feather is tickling her nose.

الريش يدغدغ أنفي.
alreesh yodghdegh anfi.

February
فبراير fobraier

The month after January is February.

الشهر التالي ليناير هو فبراير.
alshahr altali le-yanaier howa fobraier.

to feel
يشعر yash'aor

He likes to feel safe.

هو يحب أن يشعر بالأمان.
howa yoheb an yash'aor belaman.

fence
سياج seyaj

A zebra is on my fence.

الحمار الوحشي يقف على سياجي.
alhemar alwahshy yaqef 'aala seyaji.

fifteen See Numbers and Colors (page 112).
خمسة عشر khamsat 'aashr

fifty See Numbers and Colors (page 112).
خمسون khamsoon

to find
يجد yajed

He is trying to find his kite.

هو يحاول أن يجد طائرته الورقية.
howa yohawel an yajed ta-erat-teh alwaraqiea.

finger See Parts of the Body (page 114).
إصبع esba'a

fire
حريق hareeq

He can put out the fire.

يمكنه إطفاء الحريق.
yomkenoh etfa' alhareeq.

firefighter

إطفائي etfa-ee

The firefighter has boots and a hat.

الإطفائي يلبس حذاء طويل وقبعة.
aletfa-ee yalbes heza' taweel wa qoba'aa.

firefly See Insects (page 110).

حشرة اليراعة hasharat alyara'aa

firehouse

المطافئ almatafe'

Welcome to the firehouse!

مرحباً بكم في المطافئ!
marhaban bekom fe almatafe'!

first

الأول al awal

The yellow one is first in line.

الأصفر هو الأول في الصف.
alasfar howa alawal fe alsaf.

fish See Animals (page 104).

سمكة samaka

five See Numbers and Colors (page 112).

خمسة khamsa

to fix

يصلح yosleh

She wants to fix it.

هي تريد أن تصلحها.
heya toreed an tosleh-ha.

flag

راية raya

A flag is above her hat.

الراية فوق قبعتها.
alraya fawq qoba'ateha.

flat

مسطح mofatah

The tire is flat.

الإطار مسطح.
aletar mofatah.

flea See Insects (page 110).

برغوث barghooth

floor

أرضية ardiea

There is a hole in the floor.

هناك ثقب في الأرضية.
honak thoqb fe alardiea.

flower
زهرة zahra

The flower is growing.

الزهرة تنمو.
alzahra tanmo.

flute
الفلوت alfloot

Robert plays the flute.

هو يعزف على الفلوت.
howa ya'azef 'aala alfloot.

fly See Insects (page 110).
ذبابة zobaba

to fly
تطير ta-teer

The bee wants to fly.

تريد النحلة أن تطير.
toreed alnahla an tateer.

fog
ضباب dabab

He is walking in the fog.

هو يسير في الضباب.
howa yaseer fe aldabab.

food
طعام ta'aam

He eats a lot of food.

هو يأكل الكثير من الطعام.
howa ya'kol alkatheer men alta'aam.

foot See Parts of the Body (page 114).
قدم qadam

for
لأجل le-ajl

This is for you.

هذه لأجلك.
hazehi le-ajlek.

to forget
ينسى yansa

He does not want to forget his lunch!

هو لا يريد أن ينسى غدائه!
howa la yoreed an yansa ghada-eh!

fork
شوكة shawka

He eats with a fork.

هو يأكل بالشوكة.
howa ya'kol belshawka.

F

forty *See Numbers and Colors (page 112).*
أربعون arba'aoon

four *See Numbers and Colors (page 112).*
أربعة arba'a

fourteen *See Numbers and Colors (page 112).*
أربعة عشر arba'aat 'aashr

fox *See Animals (page 104).*
ثعلب tha'alb

Friday
الجمعة aljom'aa

On Friday, we go to the park.

يوم الجمعة نذهب إلى الحديقة.
yawom aljom'aa nazhab ila alhadeqa.

friend
صديق sadeeq

We are good friends.

نحن أصدقاء أعزاء.
nahno asdeqa' a'aeza'.

frog *See Animals (page 104).*
ضفدع dofda'a

front
أمام amam

She sits in front of him.

هي تجلس أمامه.
heya tajles amamoh.

fruit
فاكهة faki-ha

Fruit is delicious.

الفاكهة لذيذة.
alfaki-ha laziza.

full
ممتلئ momtale'

The cart is full of lizards.

العربة ممتلئة بالسحالي.
al'aaraba momtale'a belsahali.

fun
ممتع momte'a

She is having fun.

هي تستمتع.
heya tastamte'a.

funny
مضحك modhek

What a funny face!

ياله من وجه مضحك!
yalaho men wajh modhek!

game
لعبة **lo'aba**

We are playing a game.

نحن نلعب لعبة.
nahno nal'aab lo'aba.

garden
حديقة **hadeqa**

Roses are growing in the garden.

تنمو الورود في الحديقة.
tanmo alworood fe alhadeqa.

gate
بوابة **bawaba**

The gate is open.

البوابة مفتوحة.
albawaba maftoha.

to get
يحصل على **yah-sol 'aala**

The mice are trying to get the cheese.

تحاول الفئران أن تحصل على الجبن.
tohawel alfe'ran an tah-sol 'aala aljobn.

giraffe *See Animals (page 104).*
زرافة **zarafa**

girl
بنت **bint**

The girl is dancing.

البنت ترقص.
albint tarqos.

to give
يعطي **yo'atee**

I want to give you a present.

أريد أن أعطيك هدية.
oreed an o'ateek hadiea.

glad
مسرور **masroor**

She is glad to see you.

هي مسرورة لرؤيتك.
heya masroora le-ro'yatek.

G

G

glass
زجاج **zojaj**

Windows are made of glass.

النوافذ مصنوعة من الزجاج.
alnawafez masno'aa men alzojaj.

glasses
نظارة **nadhara**

This owl wears glasses.

هذه البومة تلبس نظارة.
hazehi alboma talbes nadhara.

gloves *See Clothing (page 106).*
قفازات **qofazat**

to go
يذهب **yazhab**

It is time to go to your room.

حان وقت الذهاب إلى الغرفة.
han waqt alzehab ila alghorfa.

goat *See Animals (page 104).*
معزاة **me'aza**

golf *See Games and Sports (page 108).*
غولف **golf**

good
جيد **jaied**

What a good dog!

ياله من كلب جيد!
halho men kalb jaied!

good-bye
مع السلامة **ma'aa assalama**

Good-bye!

مع السلامة!
ma'aa assalama!

goose
إوزة **e-weza**

A goose is riding a bicycle.

الإوزة تركب الدراجة.
ale-weza tarkab aldaraja.

gorilla

غوريلا **ghorilla**

The gorilla is eating a banana.

الغوريلا تأكل موزة.
alghorilla ta'kol mawza.

grandmother

جدتي **jadati**

My grandmother likes to bake.

تحب جدتي الخبيز.
toheb jadati alkhabeez.

to grab

يمسك بـ **yamsek be**

She wants to grab the bananas.

هي تريد أن تمسك بالموز.
heya toreed an tamsek belmawza.

grandpa

جد **jad**

Grandpa is my mom's father.

أبو أمي هو جدي.
abo omi howa Jadi.

grandfather

جد **jad**

I have fun with my grandfather!

أقضي وقتاً سعيداً مع جدي!
aqdi waqtan sa'aedan ma'aa jadi!

grape

عنب **aenab**

Get the grapes!

يصل إلى العنب!
yassel ila al'aenab!

grass

عشب **aoshb**

Cows eat grass.

البقرات تأكل العشب.
albaqara ta'kol al'aoshb.

grandma

جدّة **jada**

Grandma is my dad's mother.

أم أبي هي جدتي.
om Abi heya jadati.

grasshopper *See Insects (page 110).*

الجُندُب **aljondob**

G

gray *See Numbers and Colors (page 112).*

رمادي ramadi

great

عظيم aadheem

It is a great party.

إنها حفلة عظيمة.
yalaha men hafla 'aadhema.

green *See Numbers and Colors (page 112).*

أخضر akhdar

groceries

بقالة beqala

The groceries are falling out.

البقالة تتساقط.
albeqala ta-tasaqat.

ground

أرض ard

They live in the ground.

هم يعيشوا في الأرض.
hom ya'aeesho fe alard.

group

مجموعة majmo'aa

This is a group of artists.

هذه مجموعة من الفنانين.
hazehi majmo'aa men alfana-neen.

to grow

ينمو yanmo

He wants to grow.

هو يريد أن ينمو.
howa yoreed an yanmo.

to guess

يخمن yokhm-men

It is fun to guess what is inside.

من الممتع أن تخمن ما الذي بالداخل.
men almomte'a an tokhm-men ma al-lazi beldakhel.

guitar

غيتار gitar

My robot plays the guitar.

إنساني الآلي يعزف على الغيتار.
ensani al-ali ya'azef 'aala algitar.

hair *See Parts of the Body (page 114).*
شعر sha'ar

half نصف nesf

Half the cookie is gone.

أكلت نصف الكعكة.
akalt nesf alka'aka.

hammer مطرقة metraqa

Hit the nail with the hammer!

اطرق المسمار بالمطرقة!
etreq al mesmar belmetraqa!

hammock أرجوحة شبكية orjoha shabakiea

Dad is sleeping in the hammock.

أبي ينام في الأرجوحة الشبكية.
abi yanam fe alorjoha alshabakiea.

hand *See Parts of the Body (page 114).*
يد yad

happy سعيد sa'aeed

This is a happy face.

هذا وجه سعيد.
haza wajh sa'aeed.

hard صلب salb

The rock is hard.

الصخرة صلبة.
alsakhra salba.

harp قيثار qethar

She plays the harp very well.

هي تعزف على القيثار جيداً.
heya ta'azef 'aala alqethar jaiedan.

hat *See Clothing (page 106).*
قبعة qoba'aa

to have يملك yamlok

She needs to have three hats.

هي تريد أن تملك ثلاث قبعات.
heya toreed an tamlok thalath qoba'aat.

he هو howa

He is under the table.

هو تحت المنضدة.
howa taht almendada.

head *See Parts of the Body (page 114).*
رأس ra's

to hear *See Parts of the Body (page 114).*

يسمع yasma'a

heart

قلب qalb

The heart is red.

القلب لونه أحمر.
alqalb lawnoh ahmar.

helicopter *See Transportation (page 116).*

مروحية merwahya

hello

مرحباً marhaban

Hello. How are you?

مرحباً. كيف حالك؟
marhaban. kaif halok?

help

نجدة najda

I need help!

أحتاج إلى النجدة!
ahtaj ila alnajda!

her

لها laha

This is her tail.

هذا هو ذيلها.
haza howa zaylaha.

here

هنا hona

I live here.

أنا أعيش هنا.
ana a'aeesh hona.

hi

أهلاً ahlan

Hi!

أهلا!
ahlan!

to hide

يختبئ yakhtabe'

She is too big to hide under the box.

هي كبيرة جداً ولا يمكنها أن تختبئ تحت الصندوق.
heya kabeera jedan wala yomkenha an takhtabe' taht alsondooq.

high

مرتفع mortafe'a

The star is high in the sky.

النجم مرتفع في السماء.
alnajm mortafe'a fe alsama'.

hill

تل tl

She is coming down the hill.

هي تنزل عن التل.
heya tanzel 'aan altl.

hippopotamus See Animals (page 104).
فرس النهر faras alnahr

to hit
يضرب yadreb

He tries to hit the ball.

هو يحاول أن يضرب الكرة.
howa yohawel an yadreb alkora.

to hold
يمسك yamsek

He has to hold her hand now.

يجب أن يمسك يدها الآن.
yajeb an yamsek yadeha al-an.

hole
حفرة hofra

He is digging a hole.

هو يحفر حفرة.
howa yahfor hofra.

hooray
هتاف تشجيع
hetaf tashje'a

We are winning! Hooray!

نحن نكسب! هتاف تشجيع!
nahno naksab! hetaf tashje'a!

to hop
يحجل yahjel

They know how to hop.

هم يعرفون كيف يحجلون.
hom ya'arefon kaif yahjelon.

horse See Animals (page 104).
حصان hossan

hospital
مستشفى mostashfa

Doctors work at the hospital.

الأطباء يعملون في المستشفى.
alateba' ya'amalon fe almostashfa.

hot
ساخن sakhen

Fire is hot.

النار ساخنة.
alnar sakhena.

hotel
فندق fondoq

He is staying at
the hotel.

هو مقيم في الفندق.
howa moqeem fe alfondoq.

43

hour

ساعة sa'aa

In an hour, it is going
to be two o'clock.

بعد ساعة، ستصبح الساعة الثانية.
ba'ad sa'aa, satosbeh alsa'aa
althaniea.

house

منزل manzel

The house has many windows.

المنزل به العديد من النوافذ.
almanzel beh al'aadeed men
alnawafez.

how

كيف kaif

How does he do that?

كيف قام بهذا؟
kaif qam behaza?

hug

معانقة mo'aanaqa

Give me a hug!

عانقني!
aaneqni!

huge

ضخم dakhm

That cat is huge!

هذه القطة ضخمة!
hazehi alqeta dakhma!

hundred *See Numbers and Colors (page 112).*

مئة me-ah

(to be) hungry

جوعان jaw'aan

I think he is hungry.

أعتقد أنه جوعان.
a'ataqed anaho jaw'aan.

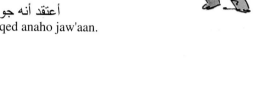

to hurry

يسرع yosre'a

She has to hurry.

يجب أن تسرع.
yajeb an tosre'a.

to hurt

تؤذي to'zi

It does not have to hurt.

يجب ألا تؤذي.
yajeb al-la to'zi.

husband

زوج zawj

He is her husband.

هو زوجها.
howa zawjoha.

I

أنا **ana**

"I am so cute!" she says.

"أنا وسيم جداً" هي قالت ذلك.
"ana wasseem jedan" heya qalat zalek.

ice

جَليد **jaleed**

We skate on ice.

نحن نتزلج على الجليد.
nahno natazalaj 'aala aljaleed.

ice cream

آيس كريم **ice cream**

She likes ice cream.

هي تحب الآيس كريم.
heya toheb al-ice cream.

idea

فكرة **fekra**

She has an idea.

هي لديها فكرة.
heya ladayha fekra.

important

مـهـم **mohem**

He looks very important.

يبدو مهماً جداً.
yabdo moheman jedan.

in

في **fe**

What is in that box?

ما الذي في الصندوق؟
ma al-lazi fe alsondooq?

inside

داخل **dakhel**

He is inside the house.

هو داخل المنزل.
howa dakhel almanzel.

into

نحو **naho**

Do not go into that cave!

لا تذهب نحو الكهف!
la tazhab naho alkahf!

island

جزيرة **jazera**

The goat is on an island.

المعزاة على الجزيرة.
alme'aza 'aala aljazera.

J

jacket *See Clothing (page 106).*
سترة sotra

jaguar *See Animals (page 104).*
نمر namer

jam مربى moraba

Do you think she likes bread and jam?

هل تعتقد أنها تحب الخبز والمربى؟
hal ta'ataqed anaha toheb alkhobz walmoraba?

January
يناير yanaier

January is the first month of the year.

يناير هو الشهر الأول في السنة.
yanaier howa alshahr alawal fe alsana.

jar مرطبان martaban

Jam comes in a jar.

المربى تأتي في المرطبان.
almoraba ta'ti fe almartaban.

job عمل aamal

It is a big job.

إنه عمل كبير.
enaho 'aamal kabeer.

juice عصير aaseer

She is pouring a glass of orange juice.

هي تصب كوباً من عصير البرتقال.
heya tasob koban men 'aaseer albortoqal.

July
يوليو yolyo

The month after June is July.

الشهر التالي ليونيو هو يوليو.
alshahr altali le-yonyo howa yolyo.

to jump
يقفز yaqfez

She loves to jump.

هي تحب أن تقفز.
heya toheb an taqfez.

June
يونيو yonyo

The month after May is June.

الشهر التالي لمايو هو يونيو.
alshahr altali le-mayo howa yonyo.

junk خردة khorda

No one can use this junk.

لا أحد يمكنه استخدام هذه الخردة.
la ahad yomkenoh estekhdam hazehi alkhorda.

kangaroo *See Animals (page 104).*

كنغر **konghr**

to keep

يحتفظ **yahtafedh**

I want to keep him.

أريد أن أحتفظ به.
oreed an ahtafedh beh.

key

مفتاح **meftah**

Which key opens the lock?

أي مفتاح يفتح القفل؟
ay meftah yaftah albab?

to kick

يركل **yar-kol**

He wants to kick the ball.

هو يريد أن يركل الكرة.
howa yoreed an yar-kol alkora.

kind

طيب **tayeb**

She is kind to animals.

هي طيبة مع الحيوانات.
heya tayeba ma'aa alhayawanat.

kind

نوع **naw'a**

What kind of animal is that?

أي نوع من الحيوانات هذا؟
ay naw'a men alhayawanat haza?

king

ملك **malek**

The king is having fun.

الملك يمرح.
almalek yamrah.

kite

طائرة ورقية

ta'era waraqya

Kites can fly high.

الطائرات الورقية تطير عالياً.
alta-erat alwaraqya ta-teer
'aalyan.

kitten

هرة **hera**

A kitten is a baby cat.

الهرة هي رضيع القطة.
alhera heya radee'a alqeta.

knee *See Parts of the Body (page 114).*

ركبة **rokba**

knife

سكين **sek-keen**

A knife can cut.

السكينة يمكن أن تقطع.
alsek-keen yomken an yaqta'a.

to knock

يقرع **yaqra'a**

He starts to knock on
the door.

هو يقرع الباب.
howa yaqra'a albab.

to know

يعرف **ya'aref**

He wants to know
what it says.

هو يريد أن يعرف ماذا تقول.
howa yoreed an ya'aref
mazal taqool.

ladder

سلم **sol-lm**

He climbs the ladder.

هو يصعد على السلم.
howa yas'aad 'aala alsol-lm.

lake

بحيرة **bohayra**

He is drinking the lake!

هو يشرب البحيرة.
howa yashrab albohayra.

lamp

مصباح **mesbah**

He has a lamp on his head.

عنده مصباح فوق رأسه.
aendaho mesbah fawq ra'seh.

lap

حجر **hejr**

He sits on his grandma's lap.

هو يجلس على حجر جدته.
howa yajles 'aala hejr jadateh.

last

الأخير **alakheer**

The pink one is last in line.

القرنفلي هو الأخير في الصف.
alqoronfoli howa alakheer fe alsaf.

late

متأخر **mota'kher**

It is late at night.

وقت متأخر من الليل.
waqt mota'akher men al-layl.

to laugh

يضحك **yadhuk**

It is fun to laugh.

من المرح أن تضحك.
men almarah an tadhuk.

lazy

كسول **kasool**

He is so lazy.

هو كسول جداً.
howa kaseel jedan.

leaf

ورقة نبات **waraqat nabat**

The tree has one leaf.

الشجرة بها ورقة واحدة.
alshajara beha waraqa waheda.

to leave
يرحل **yarhal**

She does not want to leave.

هي لا تريد أن ترحل.
heya la toreed an tarhal.

left
يسار **yassar**

This is your left hand.

هذه يدك اليسرى.
hazehi yadak alyosra.

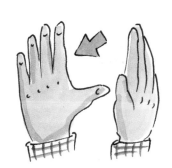

leg *See Parts of the Body (page 114).*
ساق **saq**

lemon
ليمون **laymoon**

She likes lemons.

هي تحب الليمون.
heya toheb al-laymoon.

leopard
نمر **namer**

A leopard is losing its spots.

النمر يفقد بقعه.
alnamer yafqed boqa'aeh.

to let
يترك **yatrok**

Papa is not going to let him go.

أبوه لن يتركه يذهب.
aboh ln yatrokoh yazhab.

letter
خطاب **khetab**

This letter is going airmail.

هذا الخطاب مرسل بالبريد الجوي.
haza alkhetab morsal belbareed aljawi.

library
مكتبة **Maktaba**

The library is full of books.

المكتبة ممتلئة بالكتب.
almaktaba momtale'a belkotob.

to lick
يلعق **yal'aaq**

You have to lick it.

يجب أن تلعقه.
yajeb an tal'aaqoh.

life
حياة **hayah**

Life is wonderful!

الحياة رائعة!
alhayah rae'aa!

light

ضوء daw'

The sun gives us light.

الشمس تمنحنا الضوء.
alshams tam-nah-na aldaw'.

lightning

برق barq

Look! There's lightning!

انظر! هناك برق!
ondhor! honak barq!

to like

يحب yoheb

He likes the cake.

هو يحب الكعكة.
howa yoheb alka'aka.

like

يشبه yoshbeh

She looks like a rock.

هي تشبه الصخرة.
heya toshbeh alsakhra.

line

خط khut

I can draw a line.

أنا أستطيع رسم خط.
ana astate'a rasm khut.

lion See Animals (page 104).

أسد assad

to listen

يستمع yasta-me'a

He does not want to listen to loud music.

هو لا يريد أن يستمع إلى الموسيقى الصاخبة.
howa la yoreed an yasta-me'a ila almosseqa alsakheba.

little

قصير qasseer

The bug is little.

الحشرة قصيرة.
alhashara qasseera.

to live يعيش ya'aeesh

What a nice place to live!

ياله من مكان جميل للعيش!
yalho men makan jameel lel-'aiesh!

llama See Animals (page 104).

لامة lama

to lock
يقفل **yaqfel**

Do not forget to lock the door.

لا تنسى أن تقفل الباب.
la tansa an taqfel albab.

long طويل **taweel**

That is a long snake.

هذا ثعبان طويل.
haza tho'aban taweel.

to look ينظر **yandhor**

I use this to look at the stars.

أستخدم هذا لأنظر إلى النجوم.
astakhdem haza le-andhor ila alnojoom.

to lose يفقد **yafqed**

He does not want to lose his hat.

هو لا يريد أن يفقد قبعته!
howa la yoreed an yafqed qoba'ateh!

lost
تائه **ta-eh**

Oh, no! He is lost.

لا! هو تائه.
ya ilahi! howa ta-eh.

lots
كثير **katheer**

There are lots of bubbles.

هناك الكثير من الفقاعات.
honak alkatheer men alfoqa'aat.

loud
عالي **aali**

The music is loud!

الموسيقى عالية.
almosseqa 'aalia.

to love يحب **yoheb**

She loves the present.

هي تحب الهدية.
heya toheb alhadiea.

low
منخفض **monkhafed**

The bridge is low.

الجسر منخفض.
aljesr monkhafed.

lunch غداء **ghada'**

He has nuts for lunch.

لديه بندق على الغداء.
ladieh bondoq 'aala alghada'.

mad

غاضب gha-deb

The frogs are mad.

الضفادع غاضبة.
aldafade'a ghadeba.

mail

بريد bareed

The mail is here.

البريد وصل.
albareed wassal.

mailbox

صندوق البريد
sondooq al bareed

What is in that mailbox?

ما الذي في صندوق البريد هذا؟
ma al-lazi fe sondooq albareed haza?

mail carrier

ساعي البريد
sa'ai albareed

Our mail carrier brings us the mail.

ساعي البريد يحضر لنا البريد.
sa'ai albareed yohder lana albareed.

to make

يصنع yasna'a

A belt is easy to make.

من السهل أن تصنع حزاماً.
men alsahl an tasna'a hezaman.

man

رجل rajol

The man is waving with his hand.

الرجل يلوح بيده.
alrajol yolaweh beyadeh.

mango

مانجو manjo

He will eat the whole mango.

هو سيأكل كل ثمرة المانجو.
howa saya'kol kol thamarat almanjo.

mantis See Insects (page 110).

فرس النبي faras alnabi

many

عديد aadeed

There are many dots!

هناك العديد من النقاط!
honak al'aadeed men alneqat!

map

خريطة khareeta

The map shows where to go.

توضح الخريطة طريق السير.
towadeh alkhareeta tareeq alsaier.

maraca
شخشيخة shokh-Shekha

Shake those maracas!

هز هذه الشخشيخة!
hez hazehi alshokh-shekha!

March
مارس mares

The month after February is March.

الشهر التالي لفبراير هو مارس.
alshar altali le-fobraier howa mares.

math
حساب hessab

He is not very good at math.

هو ليس جيداً في الحساب.
howa laies jayedan fe alhessab.

May
مايو mayo

The month after April is May.

الشهر التالي لأبريل هو مايو.
alshar altali le-abreel howa mares.

maybe ربما rob-bama

Maybe it is a ball.

ربما تكون كرة.
rob-bama takon kora.

mayor
محافظ mohafedh

The mayor leads the town.

المحافظ يرأس المدينة.
almohafedh yar'as almadina.

to mean
يعني ya'ani

That has to mean "hello."

هذه تعني "مرحباً".
hazehi ta'ani "marhaban".

meat لحم lahm

I am eating meat, salad, and potatoes for dinner.

أنا أكل اللحم والسلطة والبطاطس على العشاء.
ana akol al-lahm walsalata walbatates 'aala al'aasha'.

medicine
دواء dawa'

Take your medicine!

تناول دوائك!
tanawal dawa-ek!

to meet
يقابل **yoqabel**

I am happy to meet you.

أنا سعيد لمقابلتك.
ana sa'aeed le-moqa-ba-la-tek.

meow
مواء **mo-waa'**

Cats say, "MEOW!"

صوت القطط هو "المواء"!
sawt alqetat howa "almo-waa'"!

mess
فوضى **fawda**

What a mess!

يالها من فوضى!
yalaha men fawda!

messy
غير مرتب **ghayr moratab**

The bear is a little messy.

الدب غير مرتب قليلاً.
aldob ghayr moratab qalelan.

milk
حليب **haleeb**

He likes milk.

هو يحب الحليب.
howa yoheb alhaleeb.

minute
دقيقة **daqeqa**

It is one minute before noon.

تبقى دقيقة واحدة على الظهر.
tabqa daqeqa waheda 'aala aldhohr.

mirror
مرآة **mer-ah**

He loves to look in the mirror.

هو يحب النظر في المرآة.
howa yoheb alnadhar fe almer-ah.

to miss
يفوت **yofawet**

He does not want to miss the airplane.

هو لا يريد أن يفوت الطائرة.
howa la yoreed an yofawet alta-era.

mittens *See Clothing (page 106).*
قفازات صوفية **qofazat soofiea**

to mix
يخلط **yakhlt**

Use the spoon to mix it.

استخدم الملعقة للخلط.
estkhdem almel'aaqa lelkhalt.

mom
أمي **omi**

She is the baby's mom.

هي رضيعة أمي.
heya radee'at omi.

Monday
الاثنين **al-ethnien**

Every Monday we take a bath.

كل يوم اثنين نستحم.
kol youm ethnien nastahem.

money
أموال **amwal**

Look at all the money!

انظر إلى كل الأموال!
ondhor ila kol al-amwal!

monkey *See Animals (page 104).*
قرد **qerd**

month
شهر **shahr**

January and February are the first two months of the year.

يناير وفبراير أول شهرين في السنة.
yanaier wa fobraier awal shahrien fe alsana.

moon قمر **qamar**

The moon is up in the sky.

القمر مرتفع في السماء.
alqamar mortafe'a fe alsama'.

more
مزيد **mazeed**

She needs to buy more juice.

هي تحتاج إلى شراء المزيد من العصير.
heya tahtaj ila shera' almazeed men al'aaseer.

morning
صباح **sabah**

The sun comes up in the morning.

تشرق الشمس في الصباح.
tashroq alshams fe alsabah.

mosquito *See Insects (page 110).*
ناموسة **namossa**

most
معظم **mo'adham**

Most of the milk is gone.

شربت معظم الحليب.
sharebt mo'adham alhaleeb.

moth *See Insects (page 110).*
عتّة **aet-tah**

mother
أم om

She is the baby's mother.

هي رضيعة الأم.
heya radee'at al-om.

motorcycle *See Transportation (page 116).*
دراجة بخارية daraja bokha-rya

mountain جبل jabal

He is climbing up the mountain.

هو يتسلق الجبل.
howa yatassalaq al jabal.

mouse فأر fa'r

The mouse is skating.

الفأر يتزلج.
alfa'r yatazalaj.

mouth *See Parts of the Body (page 114).*
فم fm

to move
يتحرك yataharak

They have to move.

هم يجب أن يتحركوا.
hom yajeb an yata-har-rako.

movie فيلم film

They are watching a movie.

هم يشاهدون فيلماً.
hom yoshahedon filman.

Mr. السيد al saied

Say hello to Mr. Adam.

قل أهلاً للسيد آدم.
qol ahlan lel-saied Adam.

Mrs. السيدة al saieda

Mrs. Thoria is getting on the bus.

السيدة ثريا تصعد الحافلة.
alsaieda Thoria tas'aad alhafela.

much
كثير katheer

There is not much food in the refrigerator.

هناك الكثير من الطعام في الثلاجة.
honak alkatheer men alta'am fe althalaja.

music
موسيقى mosseqa

They can play music.

هم يمكنهم عزف الموسيقى.
hom yom-ken-hom 'aazf almosseqa.

nail مسمار mesmar

Try to hit the nail!

حاول طرق المسمار!
hawel tarq almesmar!

name اسم esm

His name begins with "R."

اسمه يبدأ بحرف "ر".
esmoh yabda' beharf "ra'".

neck See Parts of the Body (page 114).

رقبة raqaba

necklace
قلادة qelada

She loves her necklace.

هي تحب قلادتها.
heya toheb qela-dat-teha.

to need
يحتاج yahtaj

He is going to need a snack later.

هو سيحتاج وجبة خفيفة لاحقاً.
howa sayahtaj wajba khafefa laheqan.

neighbor
جار jar

They are neighbors.

هم جيران.
hom jeran.

nest عش aosh

The birds are near their nest.

الطيور بالقرب من عشهم.
altoyoor belqorb men 'aosh-him.

never
أبداً abadan

She is never going to fly.

هي لن تطير أبداً.
heya lan tateer abadan.

new
جديد jaded

He has a new umbrella.

لديه مظلة جديدة.
ladieh medhala jadeda.

newspaper
جريدة jareeda

Who is cutting my newspaper?

من قطع جريدتي؟
mn qata'a jareedati?

next

أقرب إلى aqrab ila

She is next to the rock.

هي أقرب إلى الصخرة.
heya aqrab ila alsakhra.

next

تالي tali

The horse is next.

الحصان هو التالي.
alhossan howa al-tali

nice

لطيف latif

What a nice clown!

ياله من مهرج لطيف!
yalho men moharej latif!

night

ليل layl

It is dark at night.

السماء مظلمة في الليل.
alsama' modhlema fe al-layl.

nine *See Numbers and Colors (page 112).*

تسعة tes'aa

nineteen *See Numbers and Colors (page 112).*

تسعة عشر tes'at 'aashr

ninety *See Numbers and Colors (page 112).*

تسعون tes'aoon

no

لا la

No, you may not go.

لا، لن تذهب.
la, ln tazhab.

noise

ضجة daja

He is making a terrible noise.

هو يصدر ضجة رهيبة.
howa yosder daja raheeba.

noisy

محدث ضجة
mohdeth daja

They are very noisy.

هم محدثون ضجة عالية.
hom mohdethon daja 'aalia.

noon

ظهر dhohr

It is noon.

هذا وقت الظهر.
haza waqt aldhohr.

N

north
الشمال alshamal

It is cold in the north.

الجو بارد في الشمال.
aljaw bared fe alshamal.

nose *See Parts of the Body (page 114).*
أنف anf

not
ليس laies

The bird is not red.

الطائر ليس أحمر اللون.
alta-er laies ahmar al-lawon.

note
ملاحظة molahadha

He is writing a note.

هو يكتب ملاحظة.
howa yaktob molahadha.

nothing
لا شيء la shay'

There is nothing in the bottle.

لا يوجد شيء في الزجاجة.
la yojad shay' fe alzojaja.

November
نوفمبر november

The month after October is November.

الشهر التالي لأكتوبر هو نوفمبر.
alshar altali le-octobar howa november.

now
الآن al-an

The mouse needs to run now.

يجب أن يجري الفأر الآن.
yajeb an yajri alfa'r al-an.

number
عدد aadad

There are five numbers.

هناك خمسة أعداد.
honak khamsat a'adad.

nurse
ممرضة momar-reda

She wants to be a nurse.

هي تريد أن تكون ممرضة.
heya toreed an takon momar-reda.

nut
جوزة jawza

I think he likes nuts.

أعتقد أنه يحب الجوز.
a'ataqed anaho yoheb aljawz.

ocean
محيط moheet

This turtle swims in the ocean.

هذه السلحفاة تسبح في المحيط.
hazehi alsolahfa tasbah fe almoheet.

o'clock
الساعة alsa'aa

It is one o'clock.

الساعة الواحدة.
alsa'aa alwaheda.

October
أكتوبر octobar

The month after September is October.

الشهر التالي لسبتمبر هو أكتوبر.
alshahr altali le-septamber howa octobar.

of
الـ al

The color of the airplane is yellow.

لون الطائرة أصفر.
lawon alta-er asfar.

oh
ياه yah

Oh! What a surprise!

ياه! يالها من مفاجأة!
yah! yalaha men mofaja'a!

old
عجوز aajooz

The alligator is very old.

التمساح عجوز جداً.
altemsah 'aajooz jedan.

on
على aala

The coat is on the chair.

المعطف على الكرسي.
alme'ataf 'aala alkorsi.

once

مرة واحدة mara waheda

Birthdays come once a year.

عيد الميلاد يأتي مرة واحدة في السنة.
aeed almelad ya'ti mara waheda
fe alsana.

one *See Numbers and Colors (page 112).*

واحد wahed

onion

بصل ba-sl

He is chopping an onion.

هو يقطع بصلة.
howa yoqate'a ba-sala.

only

فقط faqut

This is the only food left.

هذا هو الطعام المتبقي فقط.
haza howa alta'aam
almotabaqi faqut.

open

مفتوح maftooh

The window is open.

النافذة مفتوحة.
alnafeza maftohha.

or

أو aw

Do you want the red
one or the blue one?

هل تريد الحمراء أو الزرقاء؟
hal toreed alhamra' aw alzarqa'?

orange *See Numbers and Colors (page 112).*

برتقالي bortoqali

orange

برتقال bortoqal

He is squeezing oranges.

هو يعصر البرتقال.
howa yoheb 'aaseer albortoqal.

ostrich

نعامة na'aama

An ostrich can run fast.

النعامة يمكنها الجري بسرعة.
alna'aama yomkenha aljari
besor-'aa.

other
آخر akhar

What is on the other side?

ما الذي على الجانب الآخر؟
ma al-lazi 'aala aljaneb al-akhar?

oven
فرن forn

We bake cookies in an oven.

نحن نخبز الكعك في الفرن.
nahno nakhbez alka'ak fe alforn.

ouch
أه! ahh!

Ouch! That hurts!

أه! هذا مؤلم!
ahh! haza mo'lem!

over
فوق fawq

She is holding the umbrella over her head.

هي تمسك المظلة فوق رأسها.
heya tamsek almedhala fawq ra'seha.

out(side)
إلى الخارج ila alkharej

He goes out.

هو يتجه إلى الخارج.
howa yatajeh ila alkharej.

owl
بومة booma

The owl does not sleep at night.

البومة لا تنام أثناء الليل.
albooma la tanam athna' al-layl.

outdoors
في الهواء الطلق
fe alhawa' altalq

We like to play outdoors.

نحن نحب اللعب في الهواء الطلق.
nahno nal'aab fe alhawa' altalq.

to own
يمتلك yamtalek

It is wonderful to own a book.

من الرائع أن تمتلك كتاباً.
men alrae'a an tamtalek ketaban.

P

page صفحة safha

He is turning the page.

هو يقلب الصفحة.
howa yoql-leb alsafha.

paint طلاء tela'

The baby is playing with paint.

الرضيع يعبث بالطلاء.
alradee'a ya'abath beltela'.

painter
رسام rassam

He is a painter.

هو رسام.
howa rasam.

pajamas
بيجاما bejama

She is wearing pajamas to sleep.

هي تلبس البيجاما لتنام.
heya talbes albejama le-tanam.

pan
مقلاة meqla

We cook with a pan.

نحن نطهو في المقلاة.
nahno nat-ho fe almeqla.

panda
الباندا alpanda

This panda is hungry.

حيوان الباندا جائع.
hayawan alpanda ja-e'a.

pants *See Clothing (page 106).*
سروال serwal

paper ورقة waraqa

Write on the paper!

اكتب على الورقة!
oktob 'aala alwaraqa!

parent أبوان aba-wan

These parents have many babies.

هذان الأبوان عندهما الكثير
من الصغار.
hazan Aba-wan 'aenda-ho-ma alkatheer men alseghaar.

park
حديقة hadeqa

We like to go to the park.

نحن نحب الذهاب إلى الحديقة.
nahno noheb alzehab ila alhadeqa.

parrot
ببغاء babagha'

This parrot can say, "Cracker!"

هذا الببغاء يقول "أهلاً"!
haza albabagha' yaqool "ahlan"!

part جزء joz'

A wheel is part of the car.

الإطار جزء من السيارة.
aletar joz' men alsayara.

party حفلة hafla

The ants are having a party.

النمل يقيم حفلة.
alnaml yoqeem hafla.

to pat
يربت yarbet

The baby tries to pat the dog.

الرضيع يحاول أن يربت على الكلب.
alradee'a yohawel an yarbet 'aala alkalb.

paw كف kaf

He wants to shake paws.

هو يريد أن يتصافح بالكفين.
howa yoreed an yatasafah belkafien.

pea
بازلاء bazela'

He does not like to eat peas.

هو لا يحب أكل البازلاء.
howa la yoheb akl albazela'.

peach
الخوخ alkhokh

Peaches grow on trees.

الخوخ ينمو على الأشجار.
alkhokh yanmo 'aala al-ashjar.

pen
قلم qalam

The pen is leaking.

القلم يسرب.
alqalam yossareb.

pencil
قلم رصاص
qalam rassas

A pencil is for drawing.

القلم الرصاص للرسم.
alqalam alrassas lel-rasm.

penguin

بطريق batreeq

There is a penguin in your sink.

هناك بطريق في حوض الاستحمام.
honak betreeq fe hawd alestehmam.

people

أشخاص ashkhas

These people are going up.

هؤلاء الأشخاص صاعدون.
ha-ola' alashkhas sa'aedon.

pepper

فلفل أسود folfol aswad

She is using too much pepper.

هي تستخدم الكثير من الفلفل الأسود.
heya tastakhdem alkatheer men alfolfol aslwad.

peppers فلفل folfol

Peppers are good to eat.

الفلفل من النباتات الجيدة للأكل.
alfolfol men alnabatat aljaieda lel-akl.

perfume عطر aetr

She is wearing perfume.

هي تضع العطر.
heya tada'a al'aetr.

pet

حيوان أليف
hayawan aleef

This turtle is a pet.

هذه السلحفاة حيوان أليف.
hazehi alsolahfa hayawan aleef.

photograph

صورة ضوئية
sora daw'ya

Look at the photograph!

انظر إلى الصورة الضوئية!
ondhor ila alsora aldaw'ya!

piano بيانو piano

He plays the piano very well.

هو يعزف على البيانو جيداً.
howa ya'azef 'aala alpiano jaiedan.

to pick

ينتقي yantaqi

This dog likes to pick berries.

هذا الكلب يحب أن ينتقي التوت.
haza alkalb yohawel an yantaqi altoot.

picnic نزهة nozha

They are having a picnic.

هم ذاهبون في نزهة.
hom zahebon fe nozha.

picture صورة sora

This is a picture of a rabbit.

هذه صورة أرنب.
hazehi sorat arnab.

pie فطيرة fatera

Who is eating the pie?

من يأكل الفطيرة؟
mn ya'kol alfatera?

pigeon *See Animals (page 104).*
حمامة hamama

pillow
وسادة wessada

A pillow is for sleeping.

الوسادة للنوم.
alwessada lel-nawom.

ping-pong *See Games and Sports (page 108).*
تنس طاولة tenis tawla

pink *See Numbers and Colors (page 112).*
قرنفلي qoronfoli

pizza
بيتزا pitza

We like to eat pizza.

نحن نحب أكل البيتزا.
nahno noheb akl alpitza.

to place
يضع yada'a

It is good to place glasses on the nose.

من الجيد وضع النظارة على الأنف.
men aljaied wad'a alnadhara 'aala alanf.

to plan
يخطط yokhatet

It helps to plan ahead.

تساعد على التخطيط للأمام.
tosa'aed 'aala altakhteet lel-amam.

to plant يزرع yazra'a

He likes to plant nuts.

هو يحب أن يزرع الجوز.
howa yoheb an yazra'a aljawz.

to play يلعب yal'ab

Do you want to play with us?

هل تريد أن تلعب معنا؟
hal toreed an tal'aab ma'aana?

playground
ملعب **mal'aab**

Meet me at the playground!

قابلني في الملعب!
qabelni fe almal'aab!

please
من فضلك **men fadlek**

Please, feed me!

من فضلك أطعمني!
men fadlek at'aemeni!

pocket
جيب **jaieb**

What is in his pocket?

ما الذي في جيبه؟
ma al-lazi fe jaiebeh?

point
سن **sen**

It has a sharp point. Ouch!

له سن حاد. أه!
laho sen haad. ahh!

to point
يشير **yosheer**

It is not polite to point.

هو ليس مؤدباً لأنه يشير.
howa laies mo'adaban le-an-naho yosheer.

police officer
شرطي **shorti**

The police officer helps us cross the street.

الشرطي يساعدنا في عبور الطريق.
alshorti yosa'aedna fe 'aoboor altareeq.

police station
قسم الشرطة **qesm alshorta**

You can get help at the police station.

يمكنك الحصول على المساعدة في قسم الشرطة.
yomkenak alhossol 'aala almosa'aada fe qesm alshorta.

polite
مؤدب **mo'adab**

He is so polite!

هو مؤدب جداً!
howa mo'adab jedan.

pond بركة **berka**

She fell into the pond.

هي سقطت في البركة.
heya saqatat fe al berka.

poor

فقير faqeer

This poor monkey does not have much money.

هذا القرد الفقير ليس لديه الكثير من الأموال.
haza alqer alfaqeer laies ladaieh alkatheer men alamwal.

post office

مكتب البريد
maktab al bareed

Letters go to the post office.

الخطابات ترسل إلى مكتب البريد.
alkhetabat torsal ila maktab al bareed.

pot

قدر qedr

It is time to stir the pot.

حان وقت تقليب القدر.
han waqt taqleeb alqedr.

potato

بطـاطس batates

These potatoes have eyes.

ثمار البطاطس هذه لها عيون.
themar albatates hazehi laha 'aoyoon.

to pound

يطرق yatroq

Use a hammer to pound a nail.

استخدم المطرقة لطرق المسمار.
estakhdem almetraqa letarq almesmar.

present

هدية hadiea

Is the present for me?

هل الهدية من أجلي؟
hal alhadiea men ajli?

pretty

جميل hameel

It is not a pretty face.

هذا ليس وجهاً جميلاً.
haza laies wajhan jameelan.

prince

أمير amir

The prince is with his father.

الأمير مع والده.
alamir ma'aa waledoh.

princess

أميرة amira

This princess has big feet.

هذه الأميرة لها قدمان كبيران.
hazehi alamira laha qadaman kabeeran.

prize

جائزة **ja-eza**

Look who wins the prize.

انظر من فاز بالجائزة.
ondhor mn faz belja-eza.

proud

mobtahej مبتهج

She is proud of her new hat.

هي مبتهجة بقبعتها الجديدة.
heya mobtaheja beqoba-'aet-ha
aljadeda.

to pull

يسحب **yas-hab**

We're trying to pull him up.

نحن نحاول أن نسحبه لأعلى.
nahno nohawel an nas-haboh le-a'ala.

puppy

جرو **jaro**

The puppy is wet.

الجرو مبتل.
aljaro mobtal.

purple *See Numbers and Colors (page 112).*

بنفسجي **banafseji**

purse

كيس النقود

kies alnoqood

The purse is full.

كيس النقود ممتلئ.
kies alnoqood momtale'.

to push

يدفع **yadfa'a**

He needs to push hard.

يجب أن يدفع بقوة.
yajeb an yadfa'a be-qo-wa.

to put

يضع **yada'a**

Don't put your foot in
your mouth!

لا تضع قدمك في فمك!
la tada'a qadamak fe fa-mek!

puzzle

لغز **loghz**

Can you put the puzzle
together?

هل تستطيع تجميع قطع اللغز معاً؟
hal tas-ta-te'a tajmee'a qeta'a
al-loghz ma'aan?

quack
كواك quak

"Quack, quack!" sing the ducks.

البط يغني "كواك كواك"!
albat yoghani "quak quak"!

to quarrel
يتشاجر yatashajar

We do not like to quarrel.

نحن لا نحب أن نتشاجر.
nahno la noheb an nata-sha-jar.

quarter
ربع rob'a

A quarter of the pie is gone.

أكلت ربع الفطيرة.
akalt rob'a alfatera.

queen
ملكة maleka

She is queen of the zebras.

هي ملكة الحمير الوحشية.
heya malekat alhameer alwah-shaya.

question
سؤال soo-al

She has a question.

هي لديها سؤال.
heya ladayha soo-al.

quick
سريع saree'a

A rabbit is quick; a tortoise is slow.

الأرنب سريع والسلحفاة بطيئة.
alarnab saree'a walsolhfa batee-a.

quiet هادئ hade'

Shh! Be quiet!

اصمت! حافظ على الهدوء!
osmot! hafedh 'aala alhedo'!

quilt
لحاف lehaf

Who is under the quilt?

من تحت اللحاف؟
mn taht al-lehaf?

to quit ينسحب yansaheb

The raccoon wants to quit practicing.

الراكون يريد أن ينسحب من اللعبة.
alrakon yoreed an yansaheb men al-lo'aba.

quite تماماً tama-man

It is quite cold today.

الجو بارد تماماً اليوم.
aljaw bared tama-man alyawom.

R

rabbit See Animals (page 104).
أرنب arnab

race سباق sebaq
Who is going to win the race?

من سيكسب السباق؟
mn sayaksab alsebaq?

radio
مذياع mezya'a
They listen to the radio.

هم يستمعون إلى المذياع.
hom yas-ta-me-'aon ila almezya'a.

rain مطر matar
She likes the rain.

هي تحب المطر.
heya toheb almatar.

rainbow
قوس قزح qaws qazah
She is standing under a rainbow.

هي تقف تحت قوس قزح.
heya taqef taht qaws qazah.

raincoat See Clothing (page 106).
معطف المطر me'ataf al matar

raindrop
قطرات المطر
qatarat almatar
Look at the raindrops.

انظر إلى قطرات المطر.
ondhor ila qatarat almatar.

rainy ممطر momter
It's a rainy day.

إنه يوم ممطر.
enaho yawom momter.

to read
يقرأ yaqra'
Does he know how to read?

هل يعرف كيف يقرأ؟
hal ya'aref kaif yaqra'?

ready
مستعد mosta'aed
The baby is not ready to go.

الرضيع غير مستعد للخروج.
alradee'a ghayr mosta'aed lel-khoroj.

72

real

حقيقي haqi-qi

It is not a real dog.

هذا ليس كلباً حقيقياً.
haza laies kalban haqa-qiean.

really

حقاً haqan

She is really tall!

هي طويلة حقاً.
heya taweela haqan.

red *See Numbers and Colors (page 112).*

أحمر ahmar

refrigerator

ثلاجة thalaja

We keep our snowballs in the refrigerator.

نحن نحتفظ بكرات الثلج في الثلاجة.
nahno nahtafedh bekorat althalj fe althalaja.

to remember

يتذكر yatazakar

It is hard to remember his phone number.

من الصعب تذكر رقم هاتفه.
men alsa'ab tazakor raqam hatef-ho.

restaurant

مطعم mat'aam

She is eating at a restaurant.

هي تأكل في مطعم.
heya ta'kol fe almat'aam.

rice

أرز orz

Where is all the rice?

أين ذهب الأرز؟
ayn zahab al-orz?

rich

غني ghani

He is very rich.

هو غني جداً.
howa ghani jedan.

to ride

يركب yarkab

It is fun to ride a horse.

من المرح أن تركب الحصان.
men almarah an tarkab alhossan.

right

يمين yameen

This is your right hand.

هذه يدك اليمنى.
hazehi yadak alyomna.

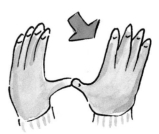

ring
خاتم khatim

She has a new ring.

لديها خاتم جديد.
ladayha khatim jaded.

robot
إنسان آلي ensan Aali

A robot is looking in my window!

الإنسان الآلي ينظر من نافذتي!
alensan al-aali yandhor men nafezati!

to ring
يدق الجرس
yadoq alja-ras

The telephone is going to ring soon.

جرس التليفون سيدق قريباً.
jaras al-hatef sa-yadoq qariban.

rock
صخرة sakhra

What is going around the rock?

ماذا يدور حول الصخرة؟
maza yadoor hawl alsakhra?

river
نهر nahr

I am floating down the river.

أنا طافية على النهر.
ana tafiya 'aala alnahr.

roof
سطح sat-h

There is a cow on the roof.

هناك بقرة فوق السطح.
honak baqara fawq alsat-h.

road
طريق tareeq

The road goes over the hill.

الطريق يصعد أعلى التل.
altareeq yas'aad a'ala al-tl.

room
غرفة ghorfa

The little house has little rooms.

المنزل الصغير به غرف صغيرة.
almanzel alsaghieer behi ghoraf saghiera.

rooster *See Animals (page 104).*

ديك deek

root

جذر jezr

The plant has deep roots.

النبات له جذور عميقة.
alnabat laho jozor 'aameqa.

rose

وردة warda

She likes roses.

هي تحب الورود.
heya toheb alworod.

round

مستدير mosta-deer

These things are round.

هذه الأشياء مستديرة.
hazehi alashya' mosta-deera.

to rub

يحك yahok

He is rubbing his tummy.

هو يحك بطنه.
howa yahok bat-neh.

rug

سجادة sejada

A bug is on the rug.

حشرة على السجادة.
hashara 'aala alsejada.

to run

يجري yajree

You need feet to run!

تحتاج إلى قدمين لتجري.
tahtaj ila qadamien le-tajree.

running *See Games and Sports (page 108).*

الجري aljarie

S

sad
حزين **hazeen**

This is a sad face.

هذا وجه حزين.
haza wajh hazeen.

sailboat *See Transportation (page 116).*
مركب شراعي **markeb she-ra-'ae**

salad
سلطة **salata**

He is making a salad.

هو يحضر السلطة.
howa yohader alsalata.

salt
ملح **melh**

She is using too much salt.

هي تستخدم الكثير من الملح.
heya tastakhdem alkatheer men almelh.

same نفس **nafs**

They look the same.

لهم نفس الشكل.
lahom nafs al-shakl.

sand رمال **remal**

There is a lot of sand
at the beach.

هناك الكثير من الرمال على الشاطئ.
honak alkatheer men alremal
'aala alshate'.

sandwich
شطيرة **shateera**

It's a pickle sandwich! Yum!

إنها شطيرة مخلل! طعمها لذيذ!
enha shaterat mokhal-lal! ta'amoha laziz!

sandy
رملي **ramli**

The beach is sandy.

الشاطئ رملي.
alshate' ramli.

Saturday
السبت **al-sabt**

On Saturday, we work
together.

يوم السبت نعمل معاً.
yawom al-sabt na'amal ma'aan.

sausage
نقانق **naqa-neq**

This dog likes sausages.

هذا الكلب يحب النقانق.
haza alkalb yoheb alnaqa-neq.

saw

منشار **menshar**

A saw is for cutting.

المنشار للقطع.
almenshar lel-qat'a.

to say

يقول **yaqool**

She wants to say hello.

هي أرادت أن تقول مرحباً.
heya aradat an taqool marhaban.

scarf *See Clothing (page 106).*

وشاح **weshah**

school

مدرسة **madrassa**

He can learn in school.

هو يتعلم في المدرسة.
howa yata'alam fe almadrassa.

scissors

مقص **mequs**

Look what he is cutting with the scissors!

أنظر ماذا يقص بالمقص!
ondhor maza yaqos belmequs!

to scrub

يفرك **yafrock**

He wants to scrub the tub.

هو يريد أن يفرك حوض الاستحمام.
howa yoreed an yafrock hawd alestehmam.

sea

بحر **bahr**

Whales live in the sea.

تعيش الحيتان في البحر.
ta'aeesh alhe-tan fe albahr.

seat

مقعد **meq'aad**

The seat is too high.

المقعد عالي جداً.
almeq'aad 'aali jedan.

secret

سر **ser**

She is telling him a secret.

هي تخبره بسر.
heya tokh-beroh be-ser.

to see *See Parts of the Body (page 114).*

يرى **yara**

seed بذرة bezra

When you plant a seed, it grows.

عندما تزرع بذرة تنمو.
aendama tazra'a bezra tanmo.

to sell يبيع yabe'a

He sells balloons.

هو يبيع البالونات.
howa yabe'a alballonat.

to send يرسل yorsel

Mom has to send a letter
in the mail.

أمي ترسل الخطاب بالبريد.
omi torsel alkhetab belbareed.

September

سبتمبر septamber

The month after August
is September.

الشهر التالي لأغسطس هو سبتمبر.
alshahr altali le-aghostos
howa september

seven See Numbers and Colors (page 112).

سبعة saba'aa

seventeen See Numbers and Colors (page 112).

سبعة عشر sab'at 'aashr

seventy See Numbers and Colors (page 112).

سبعون sab'aoon

shark قرش qersh

A shark has many teeth.

القرش له أسنان كثيرة.
alqersh laho asnan katheera.

shawl See Clothing (page 106).

شال shal

she هي heya

She is hiding.

هي تختبئ.
heya takh-ta-be'.

sheep See Animals (page 104).

خروف kharoof

shirt See Clothing (page 106).

قميص qamees

shoes See Clothing (page 106).

حذاء heza'

to shop

يتسوق yatasawaq

He likes to shop.

هو يحب أن يتسوق.
howa yoheb an yatasawaq.

short
قصير qasseer

He is too short.

هو قصير جداً.
howa qasseer jedan.

to shout
يصيح yoseeh

They have to shout.

هم يصيحون.
hom yossehoon.

shovel
مجرفة majrafa

She needs a bigger shovel.

هي تحتاج إلى مجرفة أكبر.
heya tahtaj ila majrafa akbar.

show
استعراض este'arad

They are in a show.

هم في استعراض.
hom fe este'arad.

to show
يظهر yodher

Open wide to show your new tooth!

افتح فمك تماماً لتظهر سنتك الجديدة!
eftah fa-mek tama-man le-todher senatek aljadeda!

shy
خجول khajol

He is very shy.

هو خجول جداً.
howa khajol jedan.

sick
مريض mareed

The poor rhinoceros is sick!

وحيد القرن مريض!
waheed alqarn mareed.

side جانب janeb

The tree is on the side of the house.

الشجرة إلى جانب المنزل.
alshajara ila janeb almanzel.

sidewalk
رصيف المشاة
raseef almosha

They are playing on the sidewalk.

هم يلعبون على رصيف المشاة.
hom yal'aaboon 'aala raseef almosha.

sign
إشارة eshara

This is the bakery's sign.

هذه هي إشارة المخبز.
hazehi heya esharat almakhbz.

silly

سخيف **sa-kheef**

He has a silly smile.

ضحكته سخيفة.
deh-katoh sa-kheefa.

to sing

يغني **yoghanee**

She loves to sing.

هي تحب أن تغني.
heya toheb an toghanee.

sister

أخت **okht**

They are sisters.

هم أخوات.
hom akhawat.

to sit يجلس **yajles**

They want to sit.

هم يريدون أن يجلسوا.
hom yoreedon an yajleso.

six *See Numbers and Colors (page 112).*

ستة **seta**

sixteen *See Numbers and Colors (page 112).*

ستة عشر **set-tat 'aashr**

sixty *See Numbers and Colors (page 112).*

ستون **setoon**

skateboard *See Transportation (page 116).*

لوح تزلج **laoh tazaloj**

skates *See Transportation (page 116).*

زلاجة **zalaja**

skating (ice) *See Games and Sports (page 108).*

تزلج (على الجليد) **tazaloj ('aala aljaleed)**

skiing *See Games and Sports (page 108).*

تزلج **tazaloj**

skirt *See Clothing (page 106).*

تنورة **tanoora**

sky

سماء **samaa'**

The sky is full of stars.

السماء ممتلئة بالنجوم.
alsamaa' momtale'a belnojoom.

to sleep

ينام **yanam**

He is ready to sleep.

هو مستعد للنوم.
howa mosta'aed lel-nawom.

slow

بطيء **batee'**

A rabbit is quick; a tortoise is slow.

الأرنب سريع والسلحفاة بطيئة.
alarnab saree'a walsolhfa batee-a.

small

صغير **sagheer**

An ant is small.

النملة صغيرة.
alnamla sagheera.

to smell *See Parts of the Body (page 114).*

يشم **yashom**

smile

ابتسامة **ebtessama**

What a big smile!

يالها من ابتسامة كبيرة!
yalaha men ebtessama kabeera!

smoke

دخان **dokh-khan**

Watch out for the smoke.

احذر الدخان.
ehzar aldokh-khan.

snail قوقع *qaw-qa'a*

He has a snail on his nose.

عنده قوقع في أنفه.
aendaho qaw-qa'a fe anfeh.

snake *See Animals (page 104).*

ثعبان **tho'aban**

sneakers *See Clothing (page 106).*

حذاء خفيف **heza' khafeef**

to snore

يغط في النوم
yaghot fe alnawom

Try not to snore.

حاول ألا تغط في النوم.
hawel ala taghot fe alnawom.

snow

جليد **jaleed**

Snow is white and cold.

الجليد أبيض وبارد.
aljaleed abyad wa bared.

snowball

كرة ثلج **korat thalj**

He is throwing snowballs.

هو يرمي كرات الثلج.
howa yar-me korat althalj.

so

جداً **jedan**

She is so tall!

هي طويلة جداً.
heya taweela jedan.

soap

صابون **saboon**

He is using soap to wash.

هو يستخدم الصابون في الغسيل.
howa yastakhdem alsaboon
fe alghasseel.

soccer *See Games and Sports (page 108).*

كرة قدم **korat qadam**

socks *See Clothing (page 106).*

جورب **jawrub**

sofa

أريكة **areeka**

The zebras are sitting
on the sofa.

الحمير الوحشية جالسة على الأريكة.
alhameer alwahshya jalessa 'aala
alareeka.

some

بعض **ba'ad**

Some of them are pink.

بعض منهم لونه قرنفلي.
ba'ad menhom lawonoho qoronfoli.

someday

يوماً ما **yawoman ma**

I can drive…someday.

سأستطيع القيادة...يوماً ما.
sa-astate'a alqeieada…Yawoman ma.

someone

شخص ما **shakhs ma**

Someone is behind
the fence.

شخص ما خلف السياج.
shakhs ma khalf alseyaj.

something

شيء ما **shay' ma**

Something is under the rug.

شيء ما تحت السجادة.
shay' ma taht alsejada.

song

أغنية **oghniea**

A song is for singing.

الأغنية للغناء.
aloghniea lel-ghena'.

soon

قريباً **qari-ban**

Soon it is going to be noon.

قريباً سيأتي الظهر.
qari-ban sa-ya'ti aldhohr.

sorry
آسف **aasef**

She is sorry she dropped it.

هي آسفة لأنها أسقطته.
heya aasefa le-anaha asqa-tut-ho.

soup
حساء **hessa'**

The soup is hot!

الحساء ساخن!
alhessa' sakhen!

south
الجنوب **janoob**

It is warm in the south.

الجو دافئ في الجنوب.
aljaw dafe' fe aljaboob.

special
خاص **khas**

This is a special car.

هذه سيارة خاصة.
hazehi sayara khasa.

spider
عنكبوت **aan-ka-boot**

This spider is friendly.

العنكبوت ودود.
al'aan-ka-boot wadood.

spoon
ملعقة **mel'aqa**

A spoon can't run, can it?

الملعقة لا يمكنها الجري، صحيح؟
almel'aqa la yomkenoha aljarie, saheh?

spring
الربيع **al rabee'a**

Flowers grow in spring.

الزهور تنمو في الربيع
alzohor tanmo fe alrabee'a.

square
مربع **moraba'a**

A square has four sides.

المربع له أربعة أضلاع.
almoraba'a laho araba'at ad-laa'a.

squirrel
سنجاب **senjab**

There is a squirrel on that hat.

هناك سنجاب على تلك القبعة.
honak senjab 'aala telk alqob-ba'aa.

stamp
طابع **tabe'a**

A stamp goes on a letter.

يلصق الطابع على الخطاب.
yolsaq al tabe'a 'aala alkhetab.

to stand

يقف **yaqef**

She does not like to stand.

هي لا تحب أن <u>تقف</u>.
heya la toheb an <u>taqef</u>.

star

نجم **najm**

That star is winking.

النجم يغمز.
alnajm yaghmez.

to start

يبدأ **yabd'**

They want to start with A.

هم يريدون أن يبدءوا بحرف أ.
hom yoreedon an yabda'o beharf alef.

to stay

يبقى **yabqa**

He has to stay inside.

يجب أن يبقى في الداخل.
yajeb an yabqa fe aldakhel.

to step

يخطو **yakhtoo**

Try not to step in the puddle.

حاول ألا تخطو في الوحل.
hawel ala takhtoo fe alwahl.

stick

عصا **aasa**

The dog wants the stick.

الكلب يريد العصا.
alkalb yoreed al'aasa.

sticky

لزج **lazej**

That candy is sticky.

هذه الحلوى لزجة.
hazehi alhalwa lazeja.

stomach *See Parts of the Body (page 114).*

معدة **ma'aeda**

to stop

يتوقف **yata-waqaf**

You have to stop for
a red light.

يجب أن تتوقف عند الإشارة الحمراء.
yajeb an yata-waqaf 'aend
aleshara alhamraa'.

store

متجر **matjar**

She buys books at
the store.

هي تشتري الكتب من المتجر.
heya tashtari alkotob
men almatjar.

storm

عاصفة assefa

She does not like the storm.

هي لا تحب العاصفة.
heya la toheb al'assefa.

story

قصة qesa

We all know this story.

كلنا نعرف هذه القصة.
kolona na'aref hazehi alqesa.

strange

غريب ghareeb

This is a strange animal.

هذا حيوان غريب.
haza hayawan ghareeb.

strawberry

فراولة farawla

This strawberry is big.

هذه الفراولة كبيرة.
hazehi alfarawla kabeera.

street

شارع share'a

There is an elephant in the street.

هناك فيل في الشارع.
honak feel fe alshare'a.

student

طالب taleb

The students are all fish.

الطلبة جميعهم أسماك.
altalaba jame'aahom asmak.

subway *See Transportation (page 116).*

قطار نفقي qetar nafaqi

suddenly

فجأة faj'a

Suddenly, it is raining.

السماء تمطر فجأة.
alsamaa' tomter faj'a.

suit

بذلة bazla

Something is spilling
on his suit.

شيء ما ينسكب على بذلته.
shay' ma yansakeb 'aala bazlateh.

suitcase

حقيبة سفر
haqebat safar

What is in that suitcase?

ما الذي في حقيبة السفر؟
ma al-lazi fe haqebat alsafar?

summer
الصيف alsayf

It is hot in summer.

الجو حار في الصيف.
aljaw har fe alsayf.

sun
شمس shams

The sun is hot.

الشمس ساخنة.
alshams sakhena.

Sunday
الأحد alahad

On Sunday, we eat dinner with Grandma.

يوم الأحد نتناول العشاء مع جدتنا.
yawom alahad nata-nawal al'asha' ma'aa jadatena.

sunflower
دوار الشمس
dawar alshams

The sunflower is big and yellow.

زهرة دوار الشمس كبيرة وصفراء.
zahrat dawar alshams kabeera wa safra'.

sunny
مشمس moshmess

She loves sunny days.

هي تحب الأيام المشمسة.
heya toheb alayam almoshmessa.

sure
واثق watheq

I am sure the door is not going to open.

أنا واثق أن الباب لن يفتح.
ana watheq an albab ln yoftah.

surprised
مندهش mondahesh

She is surprised.

هي مندهشة.
heya mondahesha.

sweater *See Clothing (page 106).*
سترة ثقيلة sotra thaqela

to swim
يسبح yasbah

The fish likes to swim.

السمكة تحب أن تسبح.
alsamaka toheb an tasbah.

swimming *See Games and Sports (page 108).*
سباحة sebaha

table
منضدة mendada

There is a chicken on
the table.

هناك دجاجة فوق المنضدة.
honak dajaja fawq almendada.

tail ذيل za-yl

He has a long tail.

هو لديه ذيلا طويلا.
howa ladaih za-ylan taweelan.

to take
يأخذ ya'khoz

He is going to take the
suitcase with him.

هو سيأخذ حقيبة السفر معه.
howa sa-ya'khoz haqebat
alsafar ma'aaho.

to talk
يتحدث yatahadath

They like to talk on
the phone.

هما يحبان أن يتحدثا في الهاتف.
homa yoheban an yatahadatha
fe alhatef.

tall
طويل taweel

The red one is very tall.

هذا الأحمر طويل جداً.
haza alahmar taweel jedan.

tambourine
دف dof

Shake that tambourine!

دق الدف!
doq aldof!

tan *See Numbers and Colors (page 112).*
نحاسي nohasi

to taste *See Parts of the Body (page 114).*
يتذوق yatazawaq

taxi *See Transportation (page 116).*
تاكسي taxi

teacher
معلم moa'alem

Our teacher helps us to learn.

يساعدنا المعلم على التعليم.
yosa'aedna almo'aalem 'aala
alta'aleem.

tear
دمعة dam'aa

There is a tear on her cheek.

هناك دمعة على الخد.
honak dam'aa 'aal alkhad.

telephone

هاتف hatef

People can call you on the telephone.

يمكن للأشخاص الاتصال بك
على الهاتف.
yomken lel-ashkhas aletessal bek 'aala alhatef.

television

تلفاز telfaz

My goldfish likes to watch television.

سمكتي الذهبية تحب مشاهدة التلفاز.
samakaty alzahabiea toheb moshahadet altelfaz.

to tell

يخبر yokhber

Mom has to tell her the word.

يجب أن تخبرها أمي بالكلمة.
yajeb an tokhberha omi belkalema.

ten *See Numbers and Colors (page 112).*

عشرة ashara

tennis *See Games and Sports (page 108).*

لعبة التنس lo'abat altennis

tent

خيمة khayma

What is inside the tent?

ما الذي في الخيمة؟
ma al-lazi fe alkhayma?

termite *See Insects (page 110).*

النمل الأبيض alnaml alabyad

terrible

رهيب raheeb

What a terrible mess!

يالها من فوضى رهيبة!
yalaha men fawda raheeba!

to thank

يشكر yashkor

He wants to thank the firefighter.

هو يريد أن يشكر الإطفائي.
howa yoreed an yashkor aletfa-ee.

that ذلك zalek

What is that?

ماذا يكون ذلك؟
maza yakon zalek?

their

هم hom

They are pointing to their suitcases.

هم يشيرون إلى حقائبهم.
hom yo-she-roon ila haqa'ebahom.

these

هؤلاء ha-o-laa'

No one wants these eggs.

لا أحد يريد هؤلاء الأشخاص.
la ahad yoreed ha-o-laa' alaaraneb.

them

هم hom

The shoes belong to them.

الأحذية خاصة بهم.
alahziea khassa behom.

they

هم hom

See the mice?
They are dancing.

هل ترى هذه الفئران؟
إنهم يرقصون.
hal tara hazehi alfe'ran?
enahom yarqo-soon.

then

ثم thom

Get into bed. Then sleep.

اذهب إلى السرير. ثم اخلد إلى النوم.
ezhab ila alsareer. thom okhlod ila alnawom.

thin

رفيع rafee'a

One clown is thin.

أحد المهرجين رفيع.
Ahad almoharejeen rafee'a.

there

هناك honak

She's over there.

هي هناك.
heya honak.

thing

شيء shay'

What is this thing?

ما هذا الشيء؟
ma haza alshay'?

89

to think
يفكر yofaker

We use our brain to think.

نستخدم عقلنا لنفكر.
nastakhden 'aqlana le-nofaker.

(to be) thirsty
عطشان aatshan

He is thirsty.

هو عطشان.
howa 'aatshan.

thirteen *See Numbers and Colors (page 112).*
ثلاثة عشر thalathat 'aashr

thirty *See Numbers and Colors (page 112).*
ثلاثون thalathoon

this
هذا haza

This baby is sad.

هذا الرضيع حزين.
haza alradee'a hazeen.

those
أولئك ola-eka

Those babies are happy.

أولئك الرضع سعداء.
ola-eka alroda'a so'aada'.

thousand *See Numbers and Colors (page 112).*
ألف alf

three *See Numbers and Colors (page 112).*
ثلاثة thalatha

through خلال khelal

The ball is coming through the window.

الكرة آتية من خلال النافذة.
alkora aateiea men khelal alnafeza.

to throw
يرمي yarmee

We like to throw the ball.

هو يحب أن يرمي الكرة.
howa yohawel an yarmee alkora.

thumb *See Parts of the Body (page 114).*
إبهام ebham

thunder
رعد ra'ad

Thunder is loud.

الرعد عالي الصوت.
alra'ad 'aali alsawt.

Thursday

الخميس **al khames**

On Thursday, we wash clothes.

في يوم الخميس نغسل ملابسنا.
yawom alkhames naghsel malabesna.

tie *See Clothing (page 106).*

رابطة عنق **rabetat 'aonoq**

to tie

يربط **yarbot**

Is he going to tie his shoelaces?

هل سيربط رباط الحذاء؟
hal sa-yarbot rebat alheza'?

tiger

نمر **namer**

This is a tiger.

هذا نمر.
haza namer.

time

وقت **waqt**

It is time to wash the dishes.

حان وقت غسل الأطباق.
han waqt ghasl alatbaaq.

tire

إطار **etar**

The tire is flat.

الإطار مسطح (بلا هواء).
aletar mofatah (bela hawa').

tired

مرهق **mor-haq**

She is tired.

هي مرهقة.
heya mor-haqa.

to

إلى **ila**

He is going to school.

هو ذاهب إلى المدرسة.
howa zaheb ila almadrassa.

today

اليوم **alyawom**

Today is her birthday.

اليوم عيد ميلادها.
alyawom 'aeed meladeha.

toe *See Parts of the Body (page 114).*

إصبع القدم **esba'a alqadam**

together

معاً **ma'aan**

They are sitting together.

هما جالسان معاً.
homa jalesan ma'aan.

tomato

طماطم **tamatim**

Mmm! It is a big, juicy tomato.

ياه! يالها من طماطم كبيرة
غنية بالعصير.
yah! yalaha men tamatim kabeera
ghaniea bel'aaseer.

tomorrow

غداً **ghadan**

Tomorrow is another day.

غداً يوماً آخر.
ghadan youman aakhar.

tonight

هذه الليلة **hazehi al-layla**

He is sleepy tonight.

هو ناعس هذه الليلة.
howa na'aes hazehi al-layla.

too

أيضاً **aydan**

The baby is singing, too.

الرضيع يغني أيضاً.
alradee'a yoghani aydan.

tooth *See Parts of the Body (page 114).*

سن **sen**

toothbrush

فرشاة أسنان **forshat asnan**

My toothbrush is red.

فرشاة أسناني حمراء.
forshat asnani hamra'.

top

قمة **qema**

The bird is on top.

الطائر على القمة.
alta-er 'aal alqema.

to touch *See Parts of the Body (page 114).*

يلمس **yalmes**

towel

منشفة **menshafa**

He needs a towel.

هو يحتاج منشفة.
howa yahtaj menshafa.

town

بلدة **balda**

The ant lives in a town.

يعيش النمل في البلدة.
alnaml ya'aeesh fe albalda.

toy

لعبة **lo'aba**

He has all kinds of toys.

عنده كل أنواع اللعب.
aendaho kol anwa'a al-lo'ab.

track

أثر **athr**

That is a rabbit track.

هذا أثر أرنب.
haza athr arnab.

train *See Transportation (page 116).*

قطار **qetar**

treat

دعوة **da'awa**

A bone is a treat.

دعوة على شكل عظمة.
da'awa 'aala shakl 'aadhma.

tree

شجرة **shajara**

There is a cow in that tree.

هناك بقرة على الشجرة.
honak baqara 'aala alshajara.

triangle

مثلث **mothal-lath**

A triangle has three sides.

المثلث له ثلاثة أضلاع.
almothal-lath laho thalathat ad-laa'a.

(to do) tricks

حيل **heiel**

Her job is to do tricks.

وظيفتها القيام بالحيل.
wadhefateha alqeieam belheiel.

trip

رحلة **rehla**

She is going on a trip.

هي ذاهبة في رحلة.
heya zaheba fe rehla.

to trip

يتعثر **yata'aathr**

It is not fun to trip.

شيء غير لطيف أن تتعثر.
shay' ghayer latif an tata-'aathr.

truck *See Transportation)page 116).*
شاحنة shahena

trumpet
بوق booq

This is a trumpet.

هذا بوق.
haza booq.

to try
يحاول yohawel

He tries to climb.

هو يحاول التسلق.
howa yohawel alta-saloq.

Tuesday
الثلاثاء al tholatha'

On Tuesday we wash the floors.

في يوم الثلاثاء نغسل الأرضيات.
yawom altholatha' naghsel alardieat.

tulip
زهرة التيوليب
zahrat altulip

There is a tulip on his head.

هناك زهرة تيوليب على رأسه.
honak zahrat tulip 'aala ra'seh.

to turn
يلف yalef

You have to turn it.

يجب أن تلفها.
yajeb an talefha.

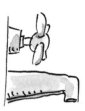

turtle
سلحفاة solahfa

That is a fast turtle!

هذه السلحفاة سريعة!
hazehi alsolahfa saree'aa!

twelve *See Numbers and Colors (page 112).*
اثنا عشر ithan 'aashr

twenty *See Numbers and Colors (page 112).*
عشرون aoshroon

twins
توأم tao-am

They are twins.

هما توأمان.
homa tao-aman.

two *See Numbers and Colors (page 112).*
اثنان ithnan

ugly
قبيح **qabeeh**

Do you think the toad is ugly?

هل تعتقد أن الضفدعة قبيحة؟
hal ta'ataqed an aldofda'a qabeeha?

umbrella
مظلة **medhala**

She has a yellow umbrella.

لديها مظلة صفراء.
ladayha medhala safra'.

uncle
عم **am**

My uncle is my dad's brother.

أخو أبي هو عمي.
akho abi howa 'aami.

under
تحت **taht**

There is something under the bed.

هناك شيء تحت السرير.
honak shay' taht alsareer.

until إلى أن **ila an**

He eats until he is full.

أكل إلى أن امتلاء
akl ila an emtala'.

up
فوق **fawq**

It's scary up here!

كم هو مخيف من فوق!
km howa mokheef men fawq!

upon
على **aala**

The box is upon the box, upon the box.

صندوق على صندوق على صندوق.
sondooq 'aala sondooq 'aala sondooq.

upside-down
مقلوب **maqloob**

He is upside-down.

هو مقلوب.
howa maqloob.

us
نا **na**

Come with us!

تعالى معنا!
ta'aala ma'aana!

to use
يستعمل **yasta'amel**

He needs to use a comb.

يحتاج أن يستعمل المشط.
yajeb an yasta'amel almesht.

V

vacation
عطلة aotla

They are on vacation.

هم في عطلة.
hom fe 'aotla.

vacuum cleaner
مكنسة كهربائية
maknassa kahroba-eiea

And here is the vacuum cleaner!

وها هي المكنسة الكهربائية!
wa ha heya almaknassa alkahroba-eiea!

van *See Transportation (page 116).*
عربة مقفلة للنقل araba moqfala lel-naql

vegetable
خضراوات khadrawat

He likes vegetables.

هو يحب الخضراوات.
howa yoheb alkhadrawat.

very
جداً jedan

It is very cold in there.

الجو بارد جداً هناك.
aljaw bared jedan honak.

vest *See Clothing (page 106).*
صُدرة sodra

veterinarian
طبيب بيطري
tabeeb baietari

A veterinarian helps animals.

الطبيب البيطري يساعد الحيوانات.
Altabeeb albaietari yosa'aed alhayawanat.

village
قرية qariea

What a pretty village!

يالها من قرية جميلة!
yalaha men qariea jameela!

violin
كمان kaman

He is playing the violin.

هو يعزف على الكمان.
howa ya'azef 'aala alkaman.

to visit
يزور yazoor

He is going to visit Grandma.

سيزور جدته.
saiezoor jedatoh.

volcano
بركان borkan

Don't go near the volcano!

لا تقترب من البركان!
la taqtareb men alborkan!

to wait
ينتظر **yantadher**

He is waiting for a bus.

هو ينتظر الحافلة.
howa yantadher alhafela.

to wake up
يستيقظ **yastayqedh**

He is about to wake up.

هو على وشك أن يستيقظ.
howa 'aala washk an yastayqedh.

to walk
يمشي **yamshi**

It is good to walk.

شيء جميل أن تمشي.
shay' jameel an tamshi.

wall
حائط **ha-et**

John is building a wall.

هو يبني حائط.
howa yabni ha-et.

warm
دافئ **dafe'**

It is warm by the fire.

الجو دافئ جانب المدفأة.
aljaw dafe' janeb almedfa'a.

to wash
يغسل **yaghsel**

It takes a long time to wash some things.

تحتاج إلى وقت طويل لغسل بعض الأشياء.
tahtaj ila waqt taweel leghasl ba'ad alashya'.

wasp
See Insects (page 110).
زنبور **zonboor**

watch
ساعة **sa'aa**

Robert is wearing his new watch.

هو يلبس ساعته الجديدة.
howa yalbes sa'atoh aljadeda.

to watch
يراقب **yoraqeb**

Peter likes to watch ants.

هو يحب أن يراقب النمل.
howa yoheb an yoraqeb alnaml.

97

water
ماء maa'

The pool is full of water.

حوض السباحة ممتلئ بالماء.
hawd alsebaha momtale' belmaa'.

we
نحن nahno

See us? We are all purple.

هل ترانا؟ نحن جميعاً باللون البنفسجي.
hal tarana? nahno jame'aan
bel-lawon albenafseji.

weather
طقس taqs

What is the weather like today?

ما حالة الطقس اليوم؟
ma halet altaqs alyawom?

Wednesday
الأربعاء alarbe'aa'

On Wednesday,
we go to work.

في يوم الأربعاء نذهب إلى العمل.
yawm alarbe'aa' nazhab ila al'aamal.

week
أسبوع asboo'a

Seven days make a week.

سبعة أيام عبارة عن أسبوع.
saba'at ayam 'aebara 'aan asboo'a.

welcome
محتفى به mohtafa beh

We are always welcome
at Grandma's house.

نحن دائماً محتفى بنا في منزل جدتي.
nahno da-eman mohtafa bena
fe manzel jedati.

well
جيداً jaiedan

Thomas builds very well.

هو يبني جيداً.
howa yabni jaiedan.

well
على ما يرام aala ma yoram

She is not well.

هي ليست على ما يرام.
heya laiesat 'aala ma yoram.

west
الغرب algharb

The sun goes down in the west.

تغرب الشمس ناحية الغرب.
taghrob alshams nahyat algharb.

wet
مبتل mobtal

William is wet.

هو مبتل.
howa mobtal.

what
ما **ma**

What is outside the window?

ما خارج النافذة؟
ma kharej alnafeza?

wheel
عجلة **ajala**

The bicycle needs a new wheel.

الدراجة تحتاج عجلة جديدة.
aldaraja tahtaj 'aajala jadeda.

when
متى **mata**

When you sleep, you close your eyes.

متى تنام تقفل عينيك.
mata tanam taqfel 'aeynaiek.

where
حيث **haith**

This is where he keeps his dinner.

هذا المكان حيث يحتفظ بعشائه.
haza almakan haith yahtafedh be'asha-eh.

which
أي **ay**

Which one do you want?

أي واحدة تريدها؟
ay waheda toreedaha?

while
أثناء **athnaa'**

I run while he sleeps.

أنا أجري أثناء نومه.
ana ajree athnaa' nawmeh.

whiskers
شعر اللحية **sha'ar al-lehya**

This animal has long whiskers.

شعر لحية هذا الحيوان طويل جداً.
sha'ar lehyat haza alhayawan taweel jedan.

to whisper
يهمس **yahmes**

This animal needs to whisper.

هذا الحيوان يهمس.
haza alhayawan yahmes.

whistle
صفارة **sofara**

They can hear the whistle.

يمكنهم سماع الصفارة.
yomkenhom sama'a alsofara.

white *See Numbers and Colors (page 112).*
أبيض **abyad**

who من **mn**

Who are you?

من أنت؟
mn ant?

whole

جميع jamee'a

Can she eat the whole thing?

هل تستطيع أكل جميع الطعام؟
hal tastate'a akl jamee'a alta'aam?

why

لماذا lemaza

Why is the baby crying?

لماذا يبكي الرضيع؟
lemaza yabkee alradee'a?

wife

زوجة zawja

She is his wife.

هي زوجته.
heya zawjatoh.

wind

ريح reeh

The wind is blowing.

تهب الريح.
tahoob alreeh.

window

نافذة nafeza

I can see through the window.

أستطيع الرؤية من خلال النافذة.
astatee'a alro'ya men khelal alnafeza.

to wink

يغمز yaghmez

It is fun to wink.

شيء مرح أن تغمز.
shay' mareh an taghmez.

winter

الشتاء al shetaa'

He skis in the winter.

هي تتزلج في الشتاء.
heya tatazalaj fe alshetaa'.

wish

أمنية omnia

The girl has a wish.

البنت عندها أمنية.
albint 'aendaha omnia.

with

مع ma'aa

The cat is dancing with the dog.

القطة ترقص مع الكلب.
alqeta tarqos ma'aa alkalb.

without

بدون bedon

He is going without his sister.

هو ذاهب بدون أخته.
howa zaheb bedon okhteh.

woman
سيدة **saieda**

My grandmother is a nice woman.

جدتي سيدة طيبة.
jadati saieda tayeba.

wonderful
مدهش **modhesh**

They are wonderful dancers.

هما راقصان مدهشان.
homa raqessan modheshan.

woods
غابة **ghaba**

Someone is walking in the woods.

شخص ما يسير في الغابة.
shakhs ma yasseer fe alghaba.

word
كلمة **kalema**

Do not say a word.

لا تقل ولا كلمة.
la taqol wala kalema.

work
عمل **aamal**

That is hard work.

هذا عمل صعب.
haza 'aamal sa'ab.

to work
يعمل **ya'amal**

She has to work hard today.

يجب أن تعمل جدياً اليوم.
yajeb an ta'amal jedyan alyawom.

world
عالم **aalam**

The world is beautiful.

العالم جميل.
al'aalam jameel.

worried
قلق **qalq**

He looks worried.

يبدو عليه القلق.
yabdo 'aalieh alqalq.

to write
يكتب **yaktob**

Katherine is trying to write with the pencil.

هي تحاول أن تكتب بالقلم الرصاص.
Heya tohawel an taktob belqalam alrassas.

wrong
خطأ **khata'**

They are putting on the wrong hats.

هما يضعان القبعتين بطريقة خطأ.
homa yada'aan alqoba-'aatan betareqa khata'.

X

X-ray
أشعة سينية ashe'aa seenya

The X-ray shows his bones.

توضح الأشعة السينية عظامه.
towadeh alashe'aa alseenya 'aedhameh.

xylophone
إكسليفون excelephone

He is a great xylophone player.

هو عازف إكسليفون ماهر.
howa 'aazef excelephone maher.

Y

yard
فناء fenaa'

There is a dinosaur in our yard.

هناك ديناصور في فنائنا.
honak dinasoor fe fenaa-ena.

yawn
تثاؤب tatha-ob

What a big yawn!

ياله من تثاؤب كبير!
halho men tatha-ob kabeer!

year
سنة sana

He runs all year.

هو يجري طوال السنة.
howa yajree towal alsana.

yellow *See Numbers and Colors (page 112).*
أصفر asfar

yes
نعم na'aam

Is he yellow? Yes! He is.

هل لونه أصفر؟ نعم! لونه أصفر.
hal lawonoho asfar? na'aam! lawonoho asfar.

yesterday
أمس ams

Yesterday is the day before today.

أمس هو اليوم الذي يسبق اليوم الحالي.
ams howa alyawom alzi yasbeq alyawom alhali.

you
أنت ant

You are reading this book.

أنت تقرأ هذا الكتاب.
ant taqra' haza alketab.

zebra
حمار وحشي **homar wahshy**

You cannot have a pet zebra!

الحمار الوحشي ليس حيواناً أليفاً!
alhemar alwahshy laies hayawanan aleefan!

zero *See Numbers and Colors (page 112).*
صفر **ciphr**

zigzag
متعرج **mota'arej**

The house has zigzags on it.

هناك خطوط متعرجة على المنزل.
honak khotot mota'areja 'aala almanzel.

to zip
يسحب السحاب
yashab alsah-hab

The bee wants to zip her jacket.

النحلة تريد سحب السحاب.
alnahala toreed sahb alsah-hab.

zipper
سحاب **sah-hab**

The zipper is stuck.

السحاب محشور.
alsah-hab mahshoor.

zoo
حديقة حيوان
hadeqat hayawan

I can see many animals at the zoo.

أرى العديد من الحيوانات في حديقة الحيوان.
ara al'aadeed men alhayawanat fe hadeqat alhayawan.

to zoom
يرتفع فجأة
yartafe'a faj'a

A rocket seems to zoom into space.

الصاروخ يرتفع فجأة إلى الفضاء.
alsarookh yartafe'a faj'a ila alfada'.

Animals
الحيوانات
alhayawanat

kangaroo
كنغر
konghr

monkey
قرد
qerd

lion
أسد
assad

elephant
فيل
feel

giraffe
زرافة
zarafa

bear
دب
dob

jaguar
نمر
namer

llama
لامة
lama

alligator
تمساح
tems-sah

snake
ثعبان
tho'aban

hippopotamus
فرس النهر
faras alnahr

fox
ثعلب
tha'alb

cow
بقرة
baqara

horse
حصان
hossan

rooster
ديك
deek

goat
معزاة
me'aza

chicken
دجاجة
dajaja

rabbit
أرنب
arnab

sheep
خروف
kharoof

pigeon
حمامة
hamama

frog
ضفدع
dofda'a

fish
سمكة
samaka

duck
بطة
bat-ta

105

Clothing

ملابس
malabes

vest
صُدرة
sodra

hat
قبعة
qoba'aa

raincoat
معطف المطر
me'ataf almatar

cap
قبعة
qoba'aa

earmuffs
أغطية الأذن
aghtiet alozon

shirt
قميص
qamees

tie
رابطة عنق
rabetat 'aonoq

jacket
سترة
sotra

pants
سروال
serwal

belt
حزام
hezam

gloves
قفازات
qofazat

socks
جورب
jawrub

sneakers
حذاء خفيف
heza' khafeef

dress
فستان
fostan

coat
معطف
me'ataf

mittens
قفازات صوفية
qofazat soofiea

scarf
وشاح
weshah

blouse
قميص
qamees

boots
أحذية
ah-zia

sweater
سترة ثقيلة
sotra thaqela

skirt
تنورة
tanoora

shoes
حذاء
heza'

shawl
شال
shal

Games and Sports
ألعاب ورياضات
al'aab wa reyadat

baseball
بيسبول
baseball

basketball
كرة سلة
korat sal-la

golf
غولف
golf

ping-pong
تنس طاولة
tenis tawla

running
الجري
aljarie

bowling
بولينغ
balling

ice skating
تزلج على الجليد
tazaloj 'aala aljaleed

soccer
كرة قدم
korat qadam

skiing
تزلج
tazaloj

tennis
لعبة التنس
lo'abat altennis

biking
ركوب الدراجة
rokob aldaraja

swimming
سباحة
sebaha

Insects
حشرات
hasharat

butterfly
فراشة
farasha

wasp
زنبور
zonboor

mantis
فرس النبي
faras al nabi

fly
ذبابة
zobaba

flea
برغوث
barghooth

beetle
خنفساء
khonfessa'

110

mosquito
ناموسة
namossa

caterpillar
يُسروع
yosro'a

grasshopper
الجُنْدُب
aljondob

moth
عتَّة
aet-tah

bee
نحلة
nahla

termite
النمل الأبيض
alnaml alabyad

firefly
حشرة اليراعة
hasharat alyara'aa

cricket
صرصار الليل
sorsar al-layl

ant
نملة
namla

111

Numbers and Colors
أعداد وألوان
a'adad wa alwan

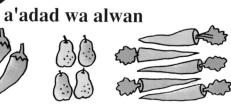

0 zero صفر
ciphr

1 one واحد
wahed

2 two اثنان
ithnan

3 three ثلاثة
thalatha

4 four أربعة
arba'a

5 five خمسة
khamsa

6 six ستة
seta

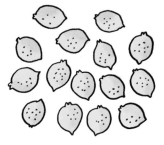

7 seven سبعة
saba'aa

8 eight ثمانية
thamania

9 nine تسعة
tes'aa

10 ten عشرة
aashara

11 eleven أحد عشر
ahad 'aashr

12 twelve اثنا عشر
ithan 'aashr

13 thirteen ثلاثة عشر
thalathat 'aashr

14 fourteen أربعة عشر
arba'aat 'aashr

15 fifteen خمسة عشر
khamsat 'aashr

16 sixteen ستة عشر
set-tat 'aashr

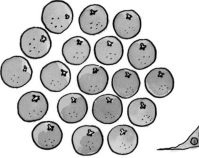
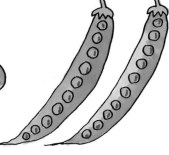

17 seventeen سبعة عشر
sab'at 'aashr

18 eighteen ثمانية عشر
thamayat 'aashr

19 nineteen تسعة عشر
tes'at 'aashr

20 twenty عشرون
aoshroon

 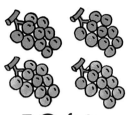  

30 thirty ثلاثون
thalathoon

40 forty أربعون
arba'aoon

50 fifty خمسون
khamsoon

60 sixty ستون
setoon

70 seventy سبعون
sab'aoon

80 eighty ثمانون
thamanoon

90 ninety تسعون
tes'aoon

100 one hundred مائة
ma'a

1000 one thousand ألف
alf

Colors

ألوان alwan

gray رمادي
ramadi

purple بنفسجي
banafseji

yellow أصفر
asfar

black أسود
aswad

green أخضر
akhdar

red أحمر
ahmar

blue أزرق
azraq

orange برتقالي
bortoqali

tan نحاسي
nohasi

brown بني
bon-nee

pink قرنفلي
qoronfoli

white أبيض
abyad

113

Parts of the Body

أجزاء الجسم
ajza' aljesm

face
وجه
wajh

head
رأس
ra's

stomach
معدة
ma'aeda

knee
ركبة
rokba

foot
قدم
qadam

leg
ساق
saq

eye
عين
ayen

thumb
إبهام
ebham

hair
شعر
sha'ar

arm
ذراع
zera'a

neck
رقبة
raqaba

finger
إصبع
esba'a

hand
يد
yad

ear
أذن
ozon

tooth
سن
sen

nose
أنف
anf

to see
يرى
yara

to touch
يلمس
yalmes

mouth
فم
fm

toe
إصبع القدم
esba'a alqadam

to hear
يسمع
yasma'a

to smell
يشم
yashom

to taste
يتذوق
yatazawaq

115

وسائل النقل

wasa-el alnaql

airplane
طائرة
ta-era

train
قطار
qetar

van
عربة مقفلة للنقل
araba moqfala lel-naql

skateboard
لوح تزلج
laoh tazaloj

bicycle
دراجة
daraja

skates
زلاجة
zalaja

116

sailboat
مركب شراعي
markeb she-ra-'ae

helicopter
مروحية
merwahya

car
سيارة
sayara

truck
شاحنة
shahena

boat
قارب
qareb

subway
قطار نفقي
qetar nafaqi

horse
حصان
hossan

taxi
تاكسي
taxi

bus
حافلة
hafela

117

Meeting and Greeting
اجتماع وتحية
ejtema'a wa tahiea

Hello!
مرحباً!
marhaban!

Hi!
أهلاً!
ahlan!

How are you?
كيف حالك؟
kaif halok?

I'm fine, thank you.
أنا بخير شكراً لك.
ana bekhaier shokran lak.

What is your name?
ما اسمك؟
ma esmok?

Ny name is Maria.
What is your name?
اسمي مروى.
ما اسمك؟
esmi Marwa. ma esmok?

My name is Susan.
اسمي هالة.
esmi Hala.

What a beautiful day!
ياله من يوم جميل!
halho men yawom jameel!

Do you live near the park?
هل تعيش بالقرب من الحديقة؟
hal ta'aeesh belqorb men alhadeqa?

Yes, I live across the street.
نعم أعيش على الجانب الآخر من الشارع.
na'aam a'aeesh 'aala aljaneb alaakhar men alshare'a.

Where do you live?
أين تعيش؟
ayn ta'aeesh?

I live on Main Street.
أعيش في الشارع الرئيسي.
a'aeesh fe alsharee'a alra-essi.

Do you know what time it is?
هل تعرف كم الساعة الآن؟
hal ta'aref km alsa'aa al-an?

It is three c'clock.
الساعة الثالثة.
alsa'aa althaletha.

Oh, I have to go now.
ياه، يجب أن أنصرف الآن.
yah, yajeb an ansaref al-an.

It was nice to meet you.
سعدت بلقائك
sa'aedt be-le-qa-ek.

Good-bye!
مع السلامة!
ma'aa assalama!

See you soon.
أراك قريبا.
arak Qari-ban.

Word List

A

a/an, 7
across, 7
add, 7
adventure, 7
afraid, 7
after, 7
again, 7
agree, 7
air, 7
airplane, 116
airport, 8
all, 8
alligator, 104
almost, 8
along, 8
already, 8
and, 8
answer, 8
ant, 110
apartment, 9
apple, 9
April, 9
arm, 114
armadillo, 9
around, 9
art, 9
as, 9
ask, 10
at, 10
August, 10
aunt, 10
awake, 10
away, 10

B

baby, 11
back, 11
bad, 11
bag, 11
bakery, 11
ball, 11
balloon, 11
banana, 11
band, 11

bandage, 11
bank, 12
barber, 12
bark, 12
baseball, 108
basket, 12
basketball, 108
bat, 12
bath, 12
be, 12
beach, 13
beans, 13
bear, 104
beautiful, 13
because, 13
bed, 13
bee, 110
beetle, 110
before, 13
begin, 13
behind, 14
believe, 14
bell, 14
belt, 106
berry, 14
best, 14
better, 14
between, 14
bicycle, 116
big, 14
biking, 108
bird, 15
birthday, 15
black, 112
blank, 15
blanket, 15
blouse, 106
blow, 15
blue, 112
boat, 116
book, 15
bookstore, 15
boots, 106
bottle, 16
bowl, 16
bowling, 108
box, 16
boy, 16
branch, 16

brave, 16
bread, 16
break, 16
breakfast, 16
bridge, 17
bring, 17
broom, 17
brother, 17
brown, 112
brush, 17
bubble, 17
bug, 17
build, 17
bus, 116
bush, 18
busy, 18
but, 18
butter, 18
butterfly, 110
button, 18
buy, 18
by, 18

C

cage, 19
cake, 19
call, 19
camel, 19
camera, 19
can, 19
candle, 19
candy, 19
cap, 106
car, 116
card, 20
care, 20
carpenter, 20
carrot, 20
carry, 20
castanets, 20
castle, 20
cat, 20
caterpillar, 110
catch, 21
cave, 21
celebrate, 21

chair, 21
chalk, 21
change, 21
cheer, 21
cheese, 21
cherry, 22
chicken, 104
child, 22
chocolate, 22
circle, 22
circus, 22
city, 22
clap, 22
class, 22
classroom, 23
clean, 23
climb, 23
clock, 23
close, 23
cloud, 23
clown, 24
coat, 106
cold, 24
comb, 24
come, 24
computer, 24
cook, 24
cookie, 24
count, 24
country, 25
cow, 104
crayon, 25
cricket, 110
crowded, 25
cry, 25
cup, 25
cut, 25
cute, 25

D

dad, 26
dance, 26
danger, 26
dark, 26
day, 26
December, 26

decide, 26
decision, 26
decorations, 26
deer, 27
dentist, 27
department, 27
desk, 27
different, 27
difficult, 27
dig, 27
dinner, 27
dinosaur, 27
dirty, 28
dish, 28
do, 28
doctor, 28
dog, 28
doll, 28
dolphin, 28
donkey, 28
door, 28
down, 28
dragon, 29
draw, 29
drawing, 29
dress, 106
drink, 29
drive, 29
drop, 29
drum, 29
dry, 29
duck, 104
dust, 29

E

each, 30
ear, 114
early, 30
earmuffs, 106
earn, 30
east, 30
eat, 30
egg, 30
eight, 112
eighteen, 112
eighty, 112
elephant, 104
eleven, 112
empty, 30
end, 31
enough, 31
every, 31

everyone, 31
everything, 31
everywhere, 31
excited, 31
eye, 114

F

face, 114
factory, 32
fall, 32
family, 32
fan, 32
far, 32
faraway, 32
fast, 32
fat, 32
father, 33
favourite, 33
feather, 33
February, 33
feel, 33
fence, 33
fifteen, 112
fifty, 112
find, 33
finger, 114
fire, 33
firefighter, 34
firefly, 110
firehouse, 34
first, 34
fish, 104
five, 112
fix, 34
flag, 34
flat, 34
flea, 110
floor, 34
flower, 35
flute, 35
fly, 35, 110
fog, 35
food, 35
foot, 114
for, 35
forget, 35
fork, 35
forty, 112
four, 112
fourteen, 112
fox, 104
Friday, 36

friend, 36
frog, 104
front, 36
fruit, 36
full, 36
fun, 36
funny, 36

G

game, 37
garden, 37
gate, 37
get, 37
giraffe, 104
girl, 37
give, 37
glad, 37
glass, 38
glasses, 38
gloves, 106
go, 38
goat, 104
golf, 108
good, 38
good-bye, 38
goose, 38
gorilla, 39
grab, 39
grandfather, 39
grandma, 39
grandmother, 39
grandpa, 39
grape, 39
grass, 39
grasshopper, 110
gray, 112
great, 40
green, 112
groceries, 40
ground, 40
group, 40
grow, 40
guess, 40
guitar, 40

H

hair, 114
half, 41
hammer, 41

hammock, 41
hand, 114
happy, 41
hard, 41
harp, 41
hat, 106
have, 41
he, 41
head, 114
hear, 114
heart, 42
helicopter, 116
hello, 42
help, 42
her, 42
here, 42
hi, 42
hide, 42
high, 42
hill, 42
hippopotamus, 104
hit, 43
hold, 43
hole, 43
hooray, 43
hop, 43
horse, 104
hospital, 43
hot, 43
hotel, 43
hour, 44
house, 44
how, 44
hug, 44
huge, 44
hundred, 112
hungry, 44
hurry, 44
hurt, 44
husband, 44

I

I, 45
ice, 45
ice cream, 45
idea, 45
important, 45
in, 45
inside, 45
into, 45
island, 45

J

jacket, 106
jaguar, 104
jam, 46
January, 46
jar, 46
job, 46
juice, 46
July, 46
jump, 46
June, 46
junk, 46

K

kangaroo, 104
keep, 47
key, 47
kick, 47
kind, 47
king, 47
kite, 48
kitten, 48
knee, 114
knife, 48
knock, 48
know, 48

L

ladder, 49
lake, 49
lamp, 49
lap, 49
last, 49
late, 49
laugh, 49
lazy, 49
leaf, 49
leave, 50
left, 50
leg, 114
lemon, 50
leopard, 50
let, 50
letter, 50
library, 50
lick, 50
life, 50

light, 51
lightning, 51
like, 51
line, 51
lion, 104
listen, 51
little, 51
live, 51
llama, 104
lock, 52
long, 52
look, 52
lose, 52
lost, 52
lots, 52
loud, 52
love, 52
low, 52
lunch, 52

M

mad, 53
mail, 53
mailbox, 53
mail carrier, 53
make, 53
man, 53
mango, 53
(praying) mantis, 110
many, 53
map, 53
maraca, 54
March, 54
math, 54
May, 54
maybe, 54
mayor, 54
me, 54
mean, 54
meat, 54
medicine, 54
meet, 55
meow, 55
mess, 55
messy, 55
milk, 55
minute, 55
mirror, 55
miss, 55
mittens, 106
mix, 55
mom, 56

Monday, 56
money, 56
monkey, 104
month, 56
moon, 56
more, 56
morning, 56
mosquito, 110
most, 56
moth, 110
mother, 57
motocycle, 116
mountain, 57
mouse, 57
mouth, 114
move, 57
movie, 57
Mr., 57
Mrs., 57
much, 57
music, 57
my, 57

N

nail, 58
name, 58
neck, 114
necklace, 58
need, 58
neighbor, 58
nest, 58
never, 58
new, 58
newspaper, 58
next, 59
nice, 59
night, 59
nine, 112
nineteen, 112
ninety, 112
no, 59
noise, 59
noisy, 59
noon, 59
north, 60
nose, 114
not, 60
note, 60
nothing, 60
November, 60
now, 60
number, 60

nurse, 60
nut, 60

O

ocean, 61
(one) o'clock, 61
October, 61
of, 61
oh, 61
old, 61
on, 61
once, 62
one, 112
onion, 62
only, 62
open, 62
or, 62
orange, 62, 112
ostrich, 62
other, 63
ouch, 63
out, 63
outdoors, 63
oven, 63
over, 63
owl, 63
own, 63

P

page, 64
paint, 64
painter, 64
pajamas, 64
pan, 64
panda, 64
pants, 106
paper, 64
parent, 64
park, 64
parrot, 65
part, 65
party, 65
pat, 65
paw, 65
pea, 65
peach, 65
pen, 65
pencil, 65
penguin, 66

people, 66
pepper, 66
peppers, 66
perfume, 66
pet, 66
photograph, 66
piano, 66
pick, 66
picnic, 66
picture, 67
pie, 67
pigeon, 104
pillow, 67
ping-pong, 108
pink, 112
pizza, 67
place, 67
plan, 67
plant, 67
play, 67
playground, 68
please, 68
pocket, 68
point, 68
police officer, 68
police station, 68
polite, 68
pond, 68
poor, 69
post office, 69
pot, 69
potato, 69
pound, 69
present, 69
pretty, 69
prince, 69
princess, 69
prize, 70
proud, 70
pull, 70
puppy, 70
purple, 112
purse, 70
push, 70
put, 70
puzzle, 70

Q

quack, 71
quarrel, 71
quarter, 71
queen, 71

question, 71
quick, 71
quiet, 71
quilt, 71
quit, 71
quite, 71

R

rabbit, 104
race, 72
radio, 72
rain, 72
rainbow, 72
raincoat, 106
raindrop, 72
rainy, 72
read, 72
ready, 72
real, 73
really, 73
red, 112
refrigerator, 73
remember, 73
restaurant, 73
rice, 73
rich, 73
ride, 73
right, 73
ring, 74
river, 74
road, 74
robot, 74
rock, 74
roof, 74
room, 74
rooster, 104
root, 75
rose, 75
round, 75
rub, 75
rug, 75
run, 75
running, 108

S

sad, 76
sailing boat, 116
salad, 76
salt, 76

same, 76
sand, 76
sandwich, 76
sandy, 76
Saturday, 76
sausage, 76
saw, 77
say, 77
scarf, 106
school, 77
scissors, 77
scrub, 77
sea, 77
seat, 77
secret, 77
see, 114
seed, 78
sell, 78
send, 78
September, 78
seven, 112
seventeen, 112
seventy, 112
shark, 78
shawl, 106
she, 78
sheep, 104
shirt, 106
shoes, 106
shop, 78
short, 79
shout, 79
shovel, 79
show, 79
shy, 79
sick, 79
side, 79
sidewalk, 79
sign, 79
silly, 80
sing, 80
sister, 80
sit, 80
six, 112
sixteen, 112
sixty, 112
skateboard, 116
skates, 116
skating (ice), 108
skiing, 108
skirt, 106
sky, 80
sleep, 80
slow, 81
small, 81

smell, 114
smile, 81
smoke, 81
snail, 81
snake, 104
sneakers, 106
snore, 81
snow, 81
snowball, 81
so, 82
soap, 82
soccer, 108
socks, 106
sofa, 82
some, 82
someday, 82
someone, 82
something, 82
song, 82
soon, 82
sorry, 83
soup, 83
south, 83
special, 83
spider, 83
spoon, 83
spring, 83
square, 83
squirrel, 83
stamp, 83
stand, 84
star, 84
start, 84
stay, 84
step, 84
stick, 84
sticky, 84
stomach, 114
stop, 84
store, 84
storm, 85
story, 85
strange, 85
strawberry, 85
street, 85
student, 85
subway, 116
suddenly, 85
suit, 85
suitcase, 85
summer, 86
sun, 86
Sunday, 86
sunflower, 86
sunny, 86

sure, 86
surprised, 86
sweater, 106
swim, 86
swimming, 108

T

table, 87
tail, 87
take, 87
talk, 87
tall, 87
tambourine, 87
tan, 112
taste, 114
taxi, 116
teacher, 87
tear, 87
telephone, 88
television, 88
tell, 88
ten, 112
tennis, 108
tent, 88
termite, 110
terrible, 88
thank, 88
that, 88
their, 89
them, 89
then, 89
there, 89
these, 89
they, 89
thin, 89
thing, 89
think, 90
thirsty, 90
thirteen, 112
thirty, 112
this, 90
those, 90
thousand, 112
three, 112
through, 90
throw, 90
thumb, 114
thunder, 90
Thursday, 91
tie, 91, 106
tiger, 91
time, 91

tire, 91
tired, 91
to, 91
today, 91
toe, 114
together, 92
tomato, 92
tomorrow, 92
tonight, 92
too, 92
tooth, 114
toothbrush, 92
top, 92
touch, 114
towel, 92
town, 93
toy, 93
track, 93
train, 116
treat, 93
tree, 93
triangle, 93
tricks, 93
trip, 93
truck, 116
trumpet, 94
try, 94
Tuesday, 94
tulip, 94
turn, 94
turtle, 94
twelve, 112
twenty, 112
twins, 94
two, 112

U

ugly, 95
umbrella, 95
uncle, 95
under, 95
until, 95
up, 95
upon, 95
upside-down, 95
us, 95
use, 95

V

vacation, 96
vacuum cleaner, 96
van, 116
vegetable, 96
very, 96
vest, 106
veterinarian, 96
village, 96
violin, 96
visit, 96
volcano, 96

W

wait, 97
wake up, 97
walk, 97
wall, 97
warm, 97
wash, 97
wasp, 110
watch, 97
water, 98
we, 98
weather, 98
Wednesday, 98
week, 98
welcome, 98
well, 98
west, 98
wet, 98
what, 99
wheel, 99
when, 99
where, 99
which, 99
while, 99
whiskers, 99
whisper, 99
whistle, 99
white, 112
who, 99
whole, 100
why, 100
wife, 100
wind, 100
window, 100
wink, 100
winter, 100
wish, 100
with, 100

without, 100
woman, 101
wonderful, 101
woods, 101
word, 101
work, 101
world, 101
worried, 101
write, 101
wrong, 101

X

X-ray, 102
xylophone, 102

Y

yard, 102
yawn, 102
year, 102
yellow, 112
yes, 102
yesterday, 102
you, 102
your, 102

Z

zebra, 103
zero, 112
zigzag, 103
zip, 103
zipper, 103
zoo, 103
zoom, 103